Studying PGCE Geography at M Level

Studying PGCE Geography at M Level is for all students undertaking their PGCE, those working to gain Masters credits and experienced teachers who wish to broaden their understanding of geography education.

Bridging the gap between theory and practice, the book is designed to support and challenge teachers as they explore geography education research, consider how theory and research enhance practice, and develop critical reflection on practice. Divided into three sections, the book:

- Investigates professional practice – what we understand about professionalism and quality in geography education and how teachers can improve their practice.
- Introduces perspectives and debates on themes and ideas in geography education including subject expertise, sustainable development, learning outside the classroom and assessment.
- Provides practical guidance on the skills involved in undertaking M level work – extended reading, engaging with theory, undertaking research and writing your dissertation.

Chapters include key readings and questions to encourage further research and reflection, and every chapter is illustrated with summaries of real students' dissertations, demonstrating the kind of research undertaken at M level.

Written by experts in geography education, *Studying PGCE Geography at M Level* offers invaluable support and inspiration for all those engaged in teaching, research and writing in geography education.

Clare Brooks is Course Leader for MA in Geography Education and Subject Leader for Geography PGCE at the Institute of Education, University of London, and a former teacher and Head of Geography.

Studying PGCE Geography at M Level

Reflection, research and writing for professional development

Edited by Clare Brooks

Routledge
Taylor & Francis Group

LONDON AND NEW YORK

First published 2010
by Routledge
2 Park Square, Milton Park, Abingdon, Oxon OX14 4RN

Simultaneously published in the USA and Canada
by Routledge
270 Madison Ave, New York, NY 10016

Routledge is an imprint of the Taylor & Francis Group, an informa business

Typeset in Bembo by Wearset Ltd, Boldon, Tyne and Wear

Printed and bound in Great Britain by TJ International, Padstow,
Cornwall

British Library Cataloguing in Publication Data
A catalogue record for this book is available from the British Library

Library of Congress Cataloging in Publication Data
Studying PGCE geography at M level : reflection, research, and
writing for professional development / edited by Clare Brooks.
p. cm.
Includes bibliographical references and index.
1. Geography teachers-Training of-Great Britain. 2. Mentoring in
education-Great Britain. I. Brooks, Clare.
G76.5.G7S78 2009
371.102--dc22

2009014408

ISBN10: (hbk) 0-415-49074-X
ISBN10: (pbk) 0-415-49075-8
ISBN10: (ebk) 0-203-86907-9

ISBN13: (hbk) 978-0-415-49074-0
ISBN13: (pbk) 978-0-415-49075-7
ISBN13: (ebk) 978-0-203-86907-9

Contents

Illustrations

Figure

Tables

Boxes

Contributors

Nicole Blum is Lecturer in Development Education at the Institute of Education, University of London.

Douglas Bourn is Director of the Development Education Research Centre at the Institute of Education, University of London, and Chair of the UNESCO UK Committee on the Decade on Education for Sustainable Development.

Clare Brooks is Course Leader for MA in Geography Education and Subject Leader for Geography PGCE at the Institute of Education, University of London, and a former teacher and Head of Geography.

Adrian Conradi is Social Studies Department Head at Dalian Maple Leaf International School, Dalian, China.

Bob Digby is Research Associate at the Institute of Education, University of London, and Community Geographer for the Geographical Association. He was previously a teacher for 24 years and has taught initial teacher education in three universities.

Karen Edge is Senior Lecturer at the London Centre for Leadership in Learning at the Institute of Education, University of London, and Principal Investigator on research projects exploring partnerships between schools in the UK, African and Asia on behalf of DfiD, British Council, PLAN and DCSF.

Denise Freeman is Head of Humanities and Subject Leader for Geography in an outer-London mixed comprehensive school.

Hakhee Kim is a research associate at the Institute of Education, University of London and a lecturer at GINUE, South Korea.

Sheila King is Director of the secondary PGCE course at the Institute of Education, University of London. She taught geography and humanities in a variety of schools in Greater London for 17 years.

David Lambert is Professor of Geography Education at the Faculty of Culture and Pedagogy, Institute of Education, University of London, and Chief Executive of the Geographical Association.

Alison Leonard is a research student at the Institute of Education, University of London, geography teacher at Westminster School, London, and lecturer at Canterbury Christ Church University for the Teach First programme.

David Mitchell is a former geography teacher and now a geography teacher educator at the Institute of Education, University of London and a consultant for the Geographical Association.

Alun Morgan is a former teacher of secondary geography and previously a lecturer in Geography Education at the Institute of Education, University of London. He is currently Director of the MSc in Education for Sustainability Programme at London South Bank University.

John Morgan is Reader in Geography Education at the Institute of Education and Graduate School of Education, University of Bristol.

Paul Weeden is Lecturer in Geography Education at the University of Birmingham and Secretary of the Assessment and Examinations Working Group of the Geographical Association.

Acknowledgements

It has become a cliché that teaching is a process of continual learning. However, having taught on the Geography PGCE and the MA in Geography Education at the Institute of Education since 2001, it is certainly true that I have learnt a great deal about teaching and learning geography through working with a range of teachers at different stages of their professional development. This book is inspired by that experience, and the authors and I are grateful to our colleagues for their inspiration.

In addition, I would like to add my personal thanks to the authors and contributors, all of whom showed outstanding commitment to this project and were generous with their time, not least in turning around drafts and meeting deadlines. I also wish to acknowledge the support and encouragement of Helen Pritt, Cat Oakley and the team at Routledge, and to all the dissertation authors and MA/PGCE students who kindly gave their permission to use their work. My thanks also go to Martin for his constant support.

Acknowledgements are gratefully expressed for permission to reprint material from the following publications:

Figure 6.1 (page 79) – Three schematic conceptualisation of sustainable development comprising three elements: economic, social and environmental, from Freeman D. and Morgan, Living in the future – education for sustainable development. In *Living Geography*. D. Mitchell (ed). London, Chris Kington Publishing, 2009, page 31.

Table 8.1 (page 106) – Developing more generalisable learning intentions, from Clarke S., *Formative Assessment in the Secondary Classroom*, London, Hodder and Stoughton, 2005.

Extract from 'An Ode to Geography' (page 144) – from Clare Madge, *Feminist Geographies: Explorations in Diversity and Difference,* by the WGSG, (1997). Permission granted by Pearson Education Ltd.

Table 13.2 (page 173) – Reading between the lines: some classic examples. Extract from *Reading between the lines: some classic examples*, Rugg, G. and Petre, M. (2004) *The Unwritten Rules of PhD Research* Open University Press 2004, Table 3, page 123.

Introduction

Clare Brooks

In 2008, the government announced that teaching was to become an all-Masters Profession (DCSF 2008). This was part of their 'Being the best for our children' initiative and was aimed at recognising the importance of a highly skilled workforce leading education. This same document also announced the MTL, a new Masters in Teaching and Learning, for teachers. Masters level education for teachers is not a new thing. Many institutions offer Masters courses in education, teaching and related fields. Since the changes in QAA guidelines, most PGCE courses now offer at least 30 Masters level credits (UCET 2006), many offer more. There are also specialist Masters courses in education, not least the MA in Geography Education offered at the Institute in Education, University of London.

The MA in Geography Education, offered at the Institute of Education, was established in 1968. When the course was developed its intention was to support geography educators in understanding the emerging field of geography education. Since then the course has developed and grown with many alumni from around the world. A distance-learning version of the course was established in 2001. Graduates of the course have made a huge impact in geography education; the alumni list stretches into government ministers, headteachers, teacher advisors, PGCE tutors, academics, as well as a long list of highly skilled, dedicated geography teachers.

I graduated from the MA in 1993. It had a significant impact on my practice, and on my subsequent career. Now, as a tutor on the course (and more recently as the Course Leader), my challenge has been to ensure that students on the course receive the same quality experience I did. The process of curriculum development has led me to question and think about what being a Master of Geography Education means, and the difficulties teachers experience whilst working towards achieving this. The fruits of that thinking have guided the preparation of this book.

Many new geography teachers will be studying at least some of their PGCE at Masters level. The challenge for those courses has been to determine what constitutes Masters level on a course which is also professional and practical. A teacher's progress on a PGCE is judged against the Standards for Qualified Teacher Status, Ofsted criteria and other benchmarks of professional judgement alongside Masters level criteria. A PGCE student has to develop their professional practice alongside their knowledge and understanding of geography education. And this is a good thing. In my experience, the more informed a teacher is, and the deeper they understand education, the more capacity they have to be 'good' at what they do. I have treated the word 'good' with caution here, because I don't want to imply that they will become the kind of teacher that I think is 'good' – but will be able to define quality in their own terms. Developing a professional position on debates such as this is a key theme running throughout this book.

And so, the purpose of this book is to offer support and challenge to geography teachers who are working at Masters level. As the title suggests, our imagined reader is someone undertaking their PGCE, or working post-PGCE to gain Masters credits in Geography Education. However, experienced geography teachers, and those not undertaking further study but wishing to broaden their understanding of geography education, will also find its contents thought-provoking and challenging. Although primarily written by authors with experience in secondary geography education in England and Wales, the contents are applicable to other sectors and contexts.

With this readership in mind, the book is divided into three parts, each reflecting one aspect of working at Masters level on a geography PGCE. The first part emphasises professional practice, exploring what we understand about professionalism and quality in geography education, and how teachers can improve their practice. The second part recognises that a geography teacher needs to engage with a range of pertinent themes and key ideas, some of which are assessed through coursework on a PGCE or Masters level course. The chapters in this part explore a range of these themes providing an introduction to the different perspectives and debates. The third part focuses on the process of undertaking Masters level work. This part emphasises academic 'skills' such as engaging with theory, undertaking research (and particularly the dissertation) and writing academic texts.

The contents of the book have been brought together to emphasise three key areas. The first of which is the link between theory and practice. As highlighted in Chapters 2, 3 and 11, teachers can have an adverse reaction to theory, somehow thinking it is difficult or irrelevant. As John Morgan suggests in Chapter 2, some teachers express concern that there is a significant difference between theory and what they do in the classroom. However, one of the intentions of this book is to demonstrate how understanding theory and research in education can enhance practice. For instance, in the first chapter, David Lambert explores how changing notions of what it means to be a professional can have a significant impact on what teachers do. Similarly, Hakhee Kim in Chapter 9 examines how the geographical content of our lessons can reflect different understandings of multiculturalism and inclusion. In each chapter, we explore relevant theory, and highlight the key readings and texts in each field, but with an emphasis on how this theory works with practice. The two go hand-in-hand.

Another key emphasis in this book is that of research. In Chapter 1, David Lambert shows that an 'activitist professional' is one that is actively engaged in constructing what they do. For geography teachers, particularly those seeking Masters level qualifications, this will involve engaging in research. For most Masters degree courses a dissertation or report is required, which constitutes a significant piece of personal research. The value of this research can be significant. Primarily, it provides a unique opportunity for a teacher to drill deep into an area that they are interested in, extending their reading into this issue, exploring alternative explanations and seeking a unique insight. As Adrian Conradi describes in Chapter 12, this can have very positive effects on a teacher's professional confidence and expertise. In addition to the personal benefits, engaging in research can lead to positive changes in the teachers' context. Alison Leonard (also in Chapter 12) demonstrates how engaging in a research project on curriculum development had far-reaching effects for the teachers, departments and students involved.

In support of this emphasis on research, each chapter seeks to encourage teachers to consider profitable avenues of research. Each chapter features a summary of a recent dissertation submitted for the MA in Geography Education. These dissertations have been carried out by students on the MA, often inspired by their experience as full-time teachers. Their inclusion in the book is for two purposes: first, to disseminate the results from some excellent practitioner research, and second, to illustrate the kind of research work that geography teachers doing Masters level work are doing. We hope you find these summaries informative and inspirational.

Each chapter also emphasises how you can go beyond their exploration covered and think more deeply about the themes in the book. Each chapter ends with some encouragement on how geography teachers can take the ideas further – either through reflection on practice, or in undertaking research. We hope that these questions will also inspire and challenge geography teachers to think about their work further.

The third emphasis in the book is to support geography teachers undertaking Masters level study in education. As such, the authors have modelled what is meant by 'argument' in educational discourse. Much work at Masters level is required to present or develop an 'argument'. However, in this context, argument means something different than its popular meaning that emphasises conflict. Here argument means showing an in-depth knowledge of the field and situating oneself within that debate. Part of undertaking Masters level study is about engaging with these professional debates. Within the academy, students are expected to demonstrate that they are familiar with proponents of each perspective and the underlying justifications for why there are different viewpoints. This can be a tricky terrain to navigate when one is getting acquainted with the field. The Western academic tradition is grounded in the Socratic dialogue – where, through dissonance, debate and disagreement, understanding is developed. We hope that the chapters in this book will encourage you to take part in this professional conversation. And so, in these chapters we have tried to model that process – demonstrating different approaches, different perspectives and often stating a preference for one side or the other. We have encouraged the reader to debate this with us – the style is not dogmatic but discursive, and as Denise Freeman suggests (in her dissertation featured in Chapter 5) the invitation is for the reader to join in the conversation.

The chapter themes represent popular areas of discussion in PGCE geography courses. In the short space allotted to each chapter, it is not always possible to explore the complexity of these themes, and so these chapters have sought to present the key ideas and key readings, and to give the reader an insight into the debate and to challenge their current thinking. Each chapter also features some areas for further reading as a starting point, should you wish to find out more about the topic in question.

As with most edited collections, this book is not meant to be read from cover to cover (although I don't want to prevent you from doing so!). The book is divided into three parts – each aimed at different outcomes and different purposes. The first part emphasises practice.

David Lambert's chapter explores what is meant by 'professional' in geography education. His chapter situates notions of professionalism within an account of how this has changed over time. He also explores what this 'new professionalism' means in practice and how a geography teacher may respond to the challenge of professional practice.

John Morgan's chapter explores what we mean by knowledge in geography teachers' practice. John explores the relationship between generic teaching advice and tips and the relationship this knowledge represents. How teacher development is understood affects the kind of guidance and support made available.

Sheila King's chapter focuses on developing the 'craft' of teaching. 'Reflective practice' is an over-used term in teaching and Sheila's chapter unpacks what it means, why it is useful and how teachers can use strategies to develop their own practice. For some there may be a tension between how teaching is 'judged' (i.e., by the QTS Standards) and how PGCE courses try to develop practice (through reflection). Sheila's chapter explores the relationship between them.

The second part of the book features seven chapters each on a topic that is relevant to both PGCE and Masters students. Many PGCE/MA courses require teachers to write about these prevalent and important themes. These writings require both reflection on practice and a detailed understanding of the literature.

The wealth of literature in education generally is huge and many of the ideas are complex. When tackling a particular topic, questions arise: what are the key ideas, who agrees with them, and why and what do others say? When reading generic education literature, the challenge can often be to identify what is the relevance particularly to geography education. This is the focus of the chapters in the middle section of the book.

Nicole Blum, Doug Bourn and Karen Edge's chapter is an introduction to the discourses in development education. Most geographers who have specialised in development studies will be familiar with the complexity of this topic, and the contrasting and contradictory ideas in the field. However, teaching about development adds an additional complexity. This chapter introduces the origins and contradictions in the field of geography education and offers some practical examples of how teachers can navigate their way through them.

Clare Brooks' chapter critically examines the role of subject expertise in teaching geography. She questions how geography teachers made decisions about what to teach, and the roles their subject knowledge and their knowledge of students play in that decision-making. An emphasis in this chapter is how thinking about the geographical content of a lesson can affect the curriculum decisions that teachers make.

Alun Morgan's chapter offers an analysis of Education for Sustainable Development and its relationship with geography education. Alun explores the different ways that sustainability and education for sustainable development can be understood. Alun also explores how teachers' understanding of this range of complex ideas can influence their practice and research.

Technology has become commonplace in classrooms generally, but especially in the geography classroom. The addition of new technologies is not unproblematic, and understanding its value, influence and contribution is still underdeveloped in geography education. David Mitchell's chapter tackles this head-on, by exploring different frameworks for why technology could make a contribution to geography education. To what extent teachers are swayed by these arguments is up to you!

The relationship between assessment and learning is one that concerns many educators. Paul Weeden's chapter is an excellent map through this complex arena. Paul clearly distinguishes between different purposes of assessment and explores their relationship to pedagogy. He demonstrates how our understanding of assessment can have profound effects on how we view teaching.

Hakhee Kim's chapter explores a controversial topic in inclusion and multiculturalism. She challenges the notion that simple steps can change how we approach inclusion, and considers how the situatedness of knowledge can help teachers to consider the positioning of their geography lessons, their students and themselves.

Fieldwork is often perceived as the domain of the geographer. How fieldwork practice has been understood has changed over time. Bob Digby traces the development of fieldwork and the influence of the changes in geography and geography education. Bob asks some challenging questions about the value of fieldwork in geography, particularly in light of the Manifesto for Learning Outside the Classroom.

Finally, the third part of the book devotes its attention to the skills of completing Masters level qualifications in education or geography education. This section is divided into three chapters, each emphasising an important dimension of what is expected of a student at this level.

First, Denise Freeman tackles theory. She takes two practical examples to show how theory is relevant to a geography teacher's practice and decision-making. Her chapter also explores the importance of understanding theory about geographical knowledge as well as theory in the field of education.

The chapter on dissertations and research has been co-written by three authors. This chapter uses Masters levels dissertations as examples of practitioner research. Clare Brooks provides background on what to consider when undertaking a dissertation, and Adrian Conradi offers a personal perspective on his dissertation journey. Alison Leonard takes a more critical view as she explores David Mitchell's research on the Geographical Association's Local Solutions project, and the impact of that research on the researcher and the participants.

The final chapter explores the difficult issue of writing at Masters level. As a graduate of geography, you will have already experienced writing graduate-level coursework. You may also have a post-graduate degree or diploma and be experienced at what is required at a post-graduate level. Despite all that experience, you may find that a PGCE at Masters level and indeed a Masters degree in education is different. In this chapter, Clare Brooks explores those differences and highlights how to overcome common pitfalls that teachers can encounter when working at Masters level.

Together we hope that the chapters in this book provide invaluable support and inspiration for geography teachers undertaking further study at Masters level. We hope you find it a rewarding experience.

References

DCSF (2008) *Being the Best for our Children: Releasing Talent for Teaching and Learning.* Department for Children, Schools and Families.

UCET (2006) *Survey Results: PGCE Qualification Levels.* Universities Council for the Education of Teachers.

Part I

Reflecting on geography teaching in practice

1 On being a professional geography teacher

David Lambert

The aims of this chapter are:

*   to open up and critically explore the nature of professionalism as it applies to teachers.
*   to distinguish different forms of professionalism in the contemporary UK context, and in particular evaluate the discourse on 'new professionalism'.
*   to argue for a form of 'activist' professionalism and briefly to discuss what this means for practice.

> You will sometimes feel you have succeeded, but disappointments will be frequent.
>
> (Michael Marland (1993) *The Craft of the Classroom*: 146)

At the end of his famous 'survival guide' for teachers, which focused on professional classroom method, Michael Marland captured what is perhaps a defining feature of *teacher* professionalism. Teaching is possibly unique, even amongst the caring professions, in being an activity that demands of its practitioners intellectual and practical engagement such that its aspirations pretty well guarantee that every day contains some measure of 'failure'. The physical and emotional load carried by teachers tends therefore to be quite heavy. It is a complex role requiring the creation and nurturing of productive relationships with a large number of adults (such as senior managers, curriculum leaders, support staff, parents who often have competing agendas and different perceptions of successful performance) and very large numbers of young people, all of whom expect individual ('personalised') attention. But the real source of tension in teaching is in trying to chart a path between the formalised policy demands on schools and teachers on the one hand, perhaps wrapped up in terms like 'performance management', and the informal cultural aspects of professionalism connected to its own 'moral purpose'.

This chapter opens up a discussion of teaching as a professional activity, with particular reference to teaching geography in primary and secondary schools in England. Particular circumstances, and the precise 'rules of engagement', vary internationally and even within the UK, but there will be much in this discussion that will translate readily to other settings.

Towards a modern professionalism

The remit of this chapter is therefore quite straightforward. Nevertheless, I approach its writing with some trepidation. Apart from the enduring difficulty of settling upon an acceptable definition of 'professional', what *tone* should one adopt? Usually, we refer to being professional as a good thing: we are often told we should strive to 'be professional', and these days this idea can be applied to most walks of life: someone who is unflappable and calm, knowledgeable and skilful, knows and operates to the rules, has dependable personal qualities (punctual, well-presented, etc.) and is fair-minded. But paradoxically, it also carries pejorative undertones. We abhor the footballer who makes a professional foul, and we sometimes sneer at some professional groups who have established such exclusive regulations and codes that they become costly and remote, living in an expensive world of their own making: think of the legal profession. To some extent such 'professional autonomy' is a myth, but to counter its negative backwash, writing on professionalism can sometimes end up sounding somewhat earnest, or overly formal and self-serving. Such writing can end up missing the mark, becoming a work of fiction in the sense that it loses touch with reality. Indeed, popular though Marland's book was and remains, it makes the professional teacher sound superhuman: even the thought of having a clear desk and clean whiteboard at the start of *every* lesson, before the children enter the room, is something that sounds unattainable!

But then how close to 'reality' should this chapter be, and whose reality? Although written in the context of the professional structures for teaching in England, which include the Professional Teaching Standards administered by the Training and Development Agency (TDA), the Teacher Learning Academy (TLA) of the General Teaching Council for England (GTCE) and the expectations and processes laid out by Ofsted in its Self Evaluation Framework (SEF), I am also aware of non-statutory and more community-based initiatives such as the Geographical Association's Geography Quality Marks and the Royal Geographical Society's Chartered Geographer (Teacher) status (you will find the web-links to all these sources at the end of this chapter). And I am also conscious of the contemporary emphasis on what, in 2004, the government called the 'new professionalism' in all public services including education, captured by this statement from the strategy unit of the Cabinet Office:

> Achieving world class services relies on innovation, consistency, continuous self-improvement and responsiveness being driven from within the public services themselves. This requires skilled and informed staff able to respond directly to the needs of the public and compare their performance with their peers
>
> (Cabinet Office 2008)

This statement from government is suggestive of 'autonomous' professional groups acting and responding locally to change – for the good of the client group. To be sure, the government does not rely solely on the inherent goodness of the professions to achieve continuous improvement, as we have already seen. There is a plethora of frameworks and regulation. But in the statement there is an admittance of the limits of centralised diktat. There is instead an invitation to 'invent' the professions locally and, within broad limits, to interpret professional roles in new ways.

We will return to the scope and potential of new localism in the next section, for what is important first of all is to analyse more closely the relationship between the external and internal aspects of teacher professionalism. Whilst I do not want to dwell too long on looking to the past, it is worth reflecting on how the idea − or ideology − of 'professional' has been constructed from its origins in the nineteenth and into the twentieth century. In fact, Michael Eraut (1994) shows how the notion of the professions is ill-defined, even the strong 'ideal-type' groups such as medicine and law. But the notion has become very influential nevertheless, fuelling arguments both for and against the role of professional power. This idea of professionalism is based upon the primacy of specialist professional knowledge and the *professionalisation* of would-be practitioners through carefully constructed selection, training and induction processes. Expert knowledge and practice, assumed to be beyond the competence of wider society whom the professions served, was developed and regulated by the profession in question. Incompetence by any members of the group was regulated and rooted out by the profession itself (self-regulation), guided by the strongly expressed ethos of public service (what used to be called 'vocation' or even a 'calling') and moral carefulness − usually in the form of a code of conduct. Eraut quotes Rueschemeyer (1983) in a way that perfectly captures this functionalist view of the professions:

> Individually and, in association, collectively, the professions 'strike a bargain with society' in which they exchange competence and integrity against the trust of client and community, relative freedom from lay supervision and interference, protection against unqualified competition as well as substantial remuneration and higher social status.
>
> (Rueschemeyer 1983: 41; cited in Eraut 1993: 3)

Teaching has struggled to measure up to this classic view of a strong profession − until very recently salaries have not been high, and nor has the social status awarded to teachers (this is, according to some analysts, related to salary levels, but is possibly also discriminatory because of the high proportion of women recruited to teaching). But there have been some other issues too. The expert knowledge base (again, until recently) has been hard to articulate and partly connected to this point, it has been very difficult to express a commercial relationship with 'clients' − especially since state education for all, in the context of the welfare state, became an established principle in the mid-twentieth century. Many teachers felt uncomfortable with the notion of being 'professional' during this era, largely because of the gap between the notion of public service and the exclusive idea of a closed, self-serving professional group (with all the possibility for arrogance that this spawned). As Craig and Fieschi (2007) observe:

> Ask a politician about teachers and they will tell you about schools – ask a teacher about themselves and they will tell you about their pupils. Teacher professionalism is inextricably linked to doing what is best for children – this is the end of teacher professionalism, it is both the motivation and the desired outcome.
>
> (2007: 2)

Thus, if there is such a thing as teacher professionalism, then it is something very different from traditional notions of 'professional', and it is very important to acknowledge and recognise this. As teaching has become increasingly recognised as a profession – with rising salaries and much more professional accountability, standards and the establishment of the General Teachers Council in 2000 – it is necessary to question what this means, not least in the context of the sustained attack the traditional professions have received during the latter years of the twentieth century (notably under Margaret Thatcher's governments). We can summarise the growing pressure on the professions as follows:

- Mounting distrust of expert, scientific and technical knowledge.
- Questions concerning whose interests professions serve (often perceived to be their own).
- Widely held suspicions about monopolies and a reluctance to join professional associations.
- Growing interest in the public voice and the rights of consumers of professional services – that is, pupils and parents.
- The establishment of 'value for money' as a key determinant of public policy, increasing the introduction of accountability measures to offset and counter 'self-regulation'.

This, then, is the context for the so-called new professionalism. Teaching as a profession has been a long-term work-in-progress, and it still is, with its members having to negotiate a complicated mixture of users and interest groups – parents, managers, policy-makers, pupils and of course the government. There are also special interest groups to take into account, often competing for attention, in the form of, for example, subject associations who often claim to offer an independent voice, and a professional 'home' for the specialist teacher. For some, like Judyth Sachs (2003), structures like these which offer professional cultures of internal control have gone some way towards preserving teachers' independence and ethics to counter government intervention and market encroachment. For many in the profession, self-regulation and autonomy are precisely the protection they need against the commercial and political forces that do not reflect their personal ethics and professional motives. However, as Craig and Fieschi show very clearly:

> this self-regulation is curtailed by the fact that it is the Secretary of State for Education who controls entry into the profession. Self-regulation, in the case of teaching, might therefore be more akin to a form of 'self-determination' – an important nuance, in particular in a situation where the professions that teachers looked to as models of professionalism are moving in different directions. . . .
>
> [However] more important than the form professionalism takes is its function. Professionalism served to negotiate boundaries between the bureaucratic rationality of public life and the personal ethical stances of teachers themselves. In this sense, professionalism served as a bridge between teachers and the society they served. . . .
>
> [But] work with teachers in our study suggested that teachers' professionalism was increasingly struggling to perform this bridging role. At times teachers expressed the sense that they were 'drowning' under the weight of public expectation and responsibility, at times they seemed to retreat from all responsibility but delivering the curriculum in classrooms. There is confusion about whether teachers owe it to society to stay up to the small hours, ironing coursework for moderators or whether they owe it to themselves to keep stricter divides between home and work. Professionalism is starting to struggle to resolve these dilemmas with any conviction and clarity between what is and is not 'down to teachers'.
>
> (2007: 9)

I think that many teachers will recognise the tension identified in this passage.

To summarise the arguments in this section, we need to emphasise two points. First, the traditional ideal–type of 'professional' is a category that teaching has always found difficult to emulate, and it is increasingly apparent that it should not even try. Those who argue that teaching has been de-professionalised with increasing government regulation are duped by a 'golden age' of professional identity that never really existed – and if it did (in some parts of the system) it was probably undesirable given the task teachers have to perform. Teaching requires a form of professionalism that functions in a way that is fit for purpose.

Second, and building on the previous point, progress has undoubtedly been made in recent years towards the creation of a stronger sense of professional identity for teaching. But in this development it is becoming clear that the profession could develop forms of *self-determination* that are responsive to external agendas but are also able to reclaim some responsibility to decide what can be done in particular circumstances and contexts. What this means, using the notion of 'new professionalism', is explored in the next section. To finish this section it is worth identifying what 'taking responsibility' does *not* mean, which is to accept professional practices uncritically, particularly those that appear not to be fit for purpose – and by this I mean something along the lines of 'moral purpose' referred to earlier. Let me illustrate.

I have been struck in recent years by how some educational organisations, including schools, seem to accept *and then magnify* codes and processes in the name of professional accountability. Preparations required for fieldwork would be a good example, whereby risk assessments as implemented by schools have sometimes become so burdensome that it has put in jeopardy the very existence of fieldwork as a component of geography education. The government's Learning Outside the Classroom initiative (www.lotc.org.uk) has attempted to address this problem from the centre, but school leadership teams and teachers themselves can take responsibility by not allowing bureaucratic concerns to override educational benefit. Similar effects can be seen at work in other aspects of school life such as assessment (e.g. the school invents sub-levels for the national curriculum) or pedagogy (e.g. *every* lesson needs a 'starter' and a 'plenary'). You will doubtless think of your own examples.

Sachs sees the tensions we have described in terms of 'managerial' and 'democratic' aspects of professionalism. However, she goes to say that

> While these two forms of teacher professionalism seem to be at either end of the spectrum, teachers' identification with them and how they impact on their work is not so oppositional. Teachers are likely to identify with either or both depending on the contexts in which they are working.
>
> (2003: 35)

Working with this tension is a good way in to consider new professionalism.

A new professionalism for teachers

Although the government introduced the idea of new professionalism in its five-year strategy published in 2004 (DfES 2004), it is a term that has been coined many times over the years. In geography education, for example, we can cite *A New Professionalism for a Changing Geography* (Hickman *et al.* 1973), a report from the Geography 14–18 Bristol Project and a title that would certainly work for 2008 given the radical reform of the curriculum at KS3. Possibly, some of its ideas would too. The curriculum 'problem' for the Project team was to initiate a programme of geography for pupils that would 'offer them an intellectually exacting study and contribute more substantially to their general education' (1973: 1). The research phase of the project identified several 'propositions' – for example, that:

- teachers need more opportunities to discuss and evaluate new ideas in geography and its teaching.
- teacher-based curriculum renewal is practical and rewarding when teachers have adequate incentive, support and feedback.

- a teacher-based approach to curriculum renewal depends on organisational support and flexibility (which is not always possible for teachers themselves to bring about).

The Geography 14–18 Project resulted in the development of teaching and learning resources, but also professional support to enable teachers 'to make curriculum renewal an integral part of their work. It [was] a policy of enhanced professionalism' (1973: 1).

Over 30 years later, the 2006–11 Action Plan for Geography (www. teachinggeographytoday.org.uk) and the Geographical Association (www. geography.org.uk) promote virtually the same idea under the guise of 'subject leadership' and identifying the subject as a resource to be used by teachers in a creative professional activity called 'curriculum making'. The key difference is that neither website talks about curriculum renewal as being part of a *new* professionalism. It is more a matter of 'reclaiming' this aspect of being a professional teacher, particularly after years of denial. Since the introduction of the national curriculum, during which time teachers were considered to be more highly skilled technicians, who *delivered* curriculum and pedagogy supported by strong managerial systems and support, rather than *making* it and thus being responsible for what is taught and accepting some level of self-determination.

Thus, if we are equating teacher professionalism with what the government seem to be encouraging – a new localism, and for teachers to combine effective managerial processes with aspects of self-determination – then there is no site more relevant for exploring this than in the making of the curriculum. Localised curriculum development may not be a 'new' idea, but we could nevertheless see how it may be the key to new professionalism now.

So what does the government have in mind when it refers to new professionalism in the early years of the twenty-first century? The following statement perhaps gives the game away:

> [Workforce reform] will usher in a new professionalism for teachers, in which career progression and financial rewards will go to those who are making the biggest contributions to improving pupil attainment, those who are continually developing their own expertise, and those who help to develop expertise in other teachers...
>
> (DfES 2004: 66)

This view of professionalism aligns very well with the Cabinet Office statement cited earlier in this chapter (page 10). It seems to heap responsibility onto teachers, and although it seems to offer possibilities for localised responsibility and a measure of self-determination, as outlined in the previous section, it is essentially managerial and linked explicitly to performance management. Central government encouragement to a 'new professionalism' therefore needs interpreting, refining and in some ways even resisting – for,

ated, the effects of such performativity could be damaging. Several groups, including the teacher unions (e.g. the ATL 2005), launched campaigns responding to the call for new professionalism. One of the most useful responses has been by the think-tank Demos, who discuss the notion of 'DIY professionalism' (Craig and Fieschi 2007), which is seen as both a threat and an opportunity. It is worth exploring this in a little detail.

In the first place, it rather turns the tables on any idea that the centre might wish to encourage local responsiveness in the profession, for the notion of 'DIY professionalism' is based on the fact that teaching *has already become* highly individualised, personal and somewhat fragmented in comparison to former, more collegial times. Not only do the structures underpinning performance such as the Professional Teaching Standards encourage individual advancement, but some of the professional support agencies have been eroded – such as the national coverage of local authority teacher advisers that existed until fairly recently. Teachers gain their professionalism increasingly through localised experience and are encouraged to seek approval and official recognition by acquiring individual reward and status – through the salary threshold to 'excellent teacher' and 'advanced skills teacher'. Further recognition of this kind can be sought (and paid for) through the subject community as with the Chartered Geographer (Teacher) status offered by the Royal Geographical Society (with the Institute of British Geographers) (RGS-IBG). To obtain and then maintain chartered status, teachers need to demonstrate a certain level of 'continuous professional development' (CPD) activity in the subject – and what we have called 'subject leadership'.

With local-authority professional-support infrastructure being in such a weakened state, the main sources of such subject-specialist CPD are now the subject organisations (principally the GA – see, for example, work under the Action Plan for Geography), the examination Awarding Bodies (who principally offer syllabus-specific advice and guidance), universities offering award-bearing CPD such as Masters courses and others such as third sector groups (e.g. FutureLab), trusts (e.g. Specialist Schools and Academies Trust) and private companies/consultants. This, again, amounts to quite a fragmented picture and even more so when we add to the list highly localised and individual initiatives, often resulting in websites and social networks of various flavours and purposes. Notable amongst these is the Staffordshire Learning Net (SLN), established by the local authority but now populated by successive waves of key individuals who keep a self-help professional conversation going, but there are many others sometimes receiving annual visitor traffic measured in millions – to put this in context, the *TES* recently estimated the number of geography teachers in the country to be around 15,000 (*TES* 2008).

It would be unimaginative to not acknowledge some of the benefits of DIY professionalism. Arguably, geography teachers have more choices and avenues for professional enhancement than ever before. But it would also be careless not to acknowledge some of the potential costs. For one thing, teachers need to be very discerning about what is on offer; for example, not to confuse the kind of support that comes through the SLN forum for CPD, in the same way as sharing 'tips for teachers' (though often useful) should not be conflated with the deeper forms of professional self-determination outlined previously. The trouble with individualism and the primacy of localised experience is, according to the Demos pamphlet, that:

> Teachers' professionalism, more than ever before, is different for different teachers. In this sense, today professionalism travels less like a broadcast and more like Chinese whispers. Here, the risk is not simply fragmentation but hidden fragmentation. The very point of Chinese whispers is not simply that the message changes, but that this change is invisible.
>
> (Craig and Fieschi 2007: 5)

The fact that teacher professionalism is informal, localised and personal means that it is reliant on network forms that are increasingly significant in school relationships. The significance of this has been recognised by those planning a national Masters in Teaching and Learning (MTL) as part of the drive to create an 'all Masters' teaching profession (announced by the Prime Minister, Gordon Brown in 2007). This is to be a practical, locally focused programme, arranged by consortia of schools and universities, and is meant to be personalised for the individual and not to be overly burdensome (and not to be a 'course' to be 'delivered'). Immediately we can again see the potential benefits and costs – and the challenge to universities to ensure notions of Masters level scholarship are maintained. However, in the context of DIY professionalism, Masters programmes have a crucial role to play in unlocking creative potential for professional renewal and development. For subject-specialist teachers, including geographers and those teaching on programmes to which geography clearly contributes (e.g. the History, Geography and Social Understanding area of learning in the primary curriculum, and some of the 14–18 Diplomas), this means a critical engagement with *curriculum* renewal and development.

The Demos pamphlet identified two consequences of DIY professionalism, the first being recognising the significance of individual, localised experience dealt with in the preceding paragraphs. The second is to acknowledge, as we hinted at earlier, that although teacher professionalism at one time simply mirrored a rather plain and straightforward education system, it must now do rather more than this, and even on occasion offer resistance – which is where the idea of self-determination becomes very important. Craig and Fieschi put it like this:

> [T]he spread of market forces through our education system seems to depend for its effectiveness on the counter-balancing force of professional norms and ethics. Schools could increasingly seek to serve narrow,

institutional interests, but the hope is that leaders' sense of 'moral purpose' will prevent this. Teachers could seek to focus solely on standards within their own classrooms, but the hope is that a sense of collegiality (itself a part of teacher professionalism) will prevent this. This is a significant new development for their professionalism. For many teachers, it creates a sense of confusion and dissonance that can lead to stress and frustration and a retreat from public norms and expectations. These vital professional norms demand and deserve explicit time and investment.

(2007: 5)

It will come as no surprise that the case being put here is one that is deployed by the General Teaching Council for England. It takes a broad view and correctly contrasts the idea of moral purpose in teaching with the narrower society and policy imperatives summed up as use of 'market forces' (which, as we have seen, imbues the government's notion of 'new professionalism') to drive up 'standards'. The idea here, crucial to sustaining and nurturing 'DIY professionalism', is that it is the collective will (indeed necessity) of teachers to persist with moral and intellectual debates that ultimately determines the aims and purposes of schools, that prevents education being utterly distorted and diminished.

Not all school communities are successful in supporting this aspect of DIY professionalism, however. For one thing, working in a school can be so intensive and *busy*, it is sometimes very difficult to lift one's eyes to perspectives from beyond the school gates. Indeed, some schools are such very inwardly oriented places ('we do it this way here') that it can seem that CPD beyond the school community is actively discouraged! Thus the GTCE is right to develop new ways to engage teachers in professional conversation and dialogue.

For geography teachers, the Geographical Association is increasingly seen as a *community of practice*, distinctive from and complementary to the *learned society* in the form of the RGS–IBG (see Gardner and Lambert 2006). A fuller discussion of this is provided in Morgan and Lambert (2005), but through its teacher conferences, projects, three journals and magazine, publications and website there is ample opportunity to keep in touch with wider debates in geography, geography education and geography teaching through membership of the Geographical Association. The GA's (2009) 'manifesto', *A Different View*, is in effect an ambitious declaration of the place of geography in education and a statement of philosophy with regard to teachers' professional development: that the geography teacher's identity and professional growth occurs through the act of curriculum development and renewal. Furthermore, that this is best done in the company of others and in the context of a wider professional dialogue – which the manifesto document is designed to stimulate. A key element of the community apparatus provided by the GA is the Geography Quality Mark (GQM). Like the RGS's Chartered Geographer

(Teacher), the GQM (which has a primary and a secondary version) was developed through the 2006–11 Action Plan for Geography. It is designed to complement chartered status for individuals, being explicitly community based and collegial – for whole primary schools or secondary school departments. Based on 'self-evaluation' procedures, the Quality Mark becomes a vehicle for teacher teams to demonstrate or develop high-quality geography programmes with colleagues. Self-evaluation activity is of course supported by an extensive 'ideas generator' provided by the GA to ensure teachers working in localised contexts are informed by wider debates and principles. The Geography Quality Mark therefore supports the GA's core principle, valuing professional development through curriculum development. In this way it supports a particular community of practice in developing the potential of DIY professionalism.

Concluding comments

In this chapter I have analysed and provided one account at least of what it means to be a 'professional' geography teacher. I have taken care to acknowledge the unsettled nature of the idea of professionalism and, in the context of our fragmented but networked society, what its significance may yet become. I have stressed the importance of 'self-determination' and, in the particular context of subject specialism, the crucial matter of curriculum making (as distinct from 'delivery').

The kind of professionalism being advocated therefore is quite similar to Judyth Sachs' notion of the 'activist' teaching profession. As she writes,

> Teacher professionalism as a concept or as a political project is not static … new forms of teacher professionalism are emerging in response to changing social, economic and political conditions. [I]t is teachers themselves in concert with various interested stakeholders who must make the intellectual, political and social running when it comes to strategies to enhance the work of teachers and the perception of the importance and status of teachers within the wider community.
>
> (2003: 6)

To conclude this chapter, it is worth summarising some of the protocols Sachs identifies as essential to underpinning the idea of the activist – creative and self-determining – professional (2003: 147–8). The activist profession needs to be:

• inclusive rather than exclusive: for me, this means at the very least to combine primary and secondary educational perspectives and to cross the academic communities of school and Higher Education where the discipline is 'made' and developed.

- collective and collaborative: this implies membership of the subject association, if only to share in the making and the promotion of a broader view (such as *A Different View*[1]).
- able to communicate aims clearly: the geography team need to have a clear sense of purpose which parents and pupils can understand – this may be helped by aligning to the GA's 'manifesto' (but of course does not need to do so).
- able to create trust and mutual respect: students are respected as learners and teachers are respected as colleagues. The formation of productive relationships lies at the core of teaching, and geography is the medium in which this happens – this is worth learning for itself but also because it contributes to the formation of the educated person.
- passionate: this takes different forms of course, and does not need to invoke images from *Dead Poets Society*. However, the professional teacher is relentless, determined and usually committed to nurturing achievement in others.

The above is not a complete listing of Sachs' protocols, and my summary may well have changed her meaning in some ways: you may judge for yourself. It is definitely worth adding that in her list there is a clear requirement for the professional teacher to experience pleasure in the role and to have fun. This is probably vital to ensure that the pupils have fun, and it is a useful way of reminding ourselves always to keep the essential managerial functions that inhabit teaching in their place.

Dissertation summary

A good many, if not the vast majority, of MA dissertations could be used to illustrate 'professionalism' in geography teaching. After all, conducting a personal research study in an aspect of your work is in itself a sign of activist professionalism. This is true whether the dissertation is a small-scale empirical study, a piece of targeted action research or a conceptual discussion on the aims of geography education.

The value of such work is felt chiefly by the person undertaking it: that is, the reading, the deep thought about what the research is meant to achieve and how best to undertake it (in the time allowed!). However, research can be reported in various ways to wider audiences – via journals such as *Geography* and *Teaching Geography* and websites such as GeogEd (via www.geography.org.uk/gtip).

And, of course, undertaking research deepens, informs, extends – and muddies – your grasp of geography in education and geography teaching. This provides you with a valuable resource to draw from in professional conversations with colleagues for the rest of your professional life. It also teaches you the good habits of healthy scepticism: the very basis of an autonomous professional.

For discussion

- Do you agree with the assertion made in this chapter that schools can sometimes be very 'inward-looking places'? How important is it in your view to adopt a broadly based, informed view of education and the teaching of geography – such as that which comes through 'active' membership of a specialist community of practice?
- What are the pros and cons of describing teaching as a profession?
- Explore the meaning and the potential benefits of DIY professionalism for you, and the impact this may have on the geography curriculum.

Further reading

1 The Teacher Training Resource Bank (www.ttrb.ac.uk) is a fine place to begin a wider investigation into professionalism as it applies to teaching. There are hundreds of articles that touch on the issue of professionalism.
2 Carr, D. (2004) *Professionalism and Ethics in Teaching*, London: Routledge, is a book well worth spending some time with, for it sets out and extends some of the arguments in this chapter – notably the tensions that exist between forms of professionalism.
3 In Day, C. (2004) *A Passion for Teaching*, London: RoutledgeFalmer, the author also presents a case grounded in the moral purpose of teaching. This is a book that identifies what drives teaching. It lays bare the obsession with 'effectiveness' and 'what works' that sometimes overwhelms us, literally getting in the way of the spirit and emotional engagement that are every bit as important to teaching as intellectual challenge and good management.

Note

1 This title is not meant to suggest a 'different' school geography. It simply evokes the notion that we see the world from different perspectives and geography as a discipline recognises this. It also evokes the philosopher's idea that to educate does not mean to arrive but 'to travel with a different view' (Peters 1963).

References

ATL (2005) *New Professionalism*. Online, available at: www.atl.org.uk/policy-and-campaigns/policies/new-professionalism.asp.

Cabinet Office (2008) *New Professionalism*. Online, available at: www.cabinetoffice.gov.uk/strategy/publications/excellence_and_fairness/professionalism.aspx.

Craig, J. and Fieschi, C. (2007) *DIY Professionalism: Futures for Teaching*, Demos in association with GTC.

DfES (2004) *Department for Education and Skills: Five-year Strategy for Children and Learners*. Online, available at: www.teachernet.gov.uk/educationoverview/briefing/strategyarchive/dfes5yearstrategy.

Eraut, M. (1994) *Developing Professional Knowledge and Competence*, Sussex: Falmer Press.

Gardner, R. and Lambert, D. (2006) 'The role of subject associations', *Geography* 91, 2, 159–71.

General Teaching Council for England (GTCE) (n.d.) Teacher Learning Academy. Online, available at: www.gtce.org.uk/tla.

Geography Teaching Today (n.d.) Chartered Geographer (Teacher) (RGS-IBG). Online, available at: www.geographyteachingtoday.org.uk/chartered-geographer/introduction.

Geography Teaching Today (n.d.) Geography Quality Marks (GA). Online, available at: www.geographyteachingtoday.org.uk/quality-marks/introduction.

Geographical Association (2009) *A Different View: a Manifesto from the Geographical Association*, Sheffield: Geographical Association.

Hickman, G., Reynolds, J. and Tolley, H. (1973) *A New Professionalism for a Changing Geography*, Schools Council Geography 14–18 Project: Schools Council.

Marland, M. (1993) *The Craft of the Classroom*, Oxford: Heinemann.

Morgan, J. and Lambert, D. (2005) *Teaching School Subjects: Geography*, London: Routledge.

Ofsted (n.d.) Self-Evaluation Form. Online, available at: www.ofsted.gov.uk/Ofsted-home/Forms-and-guidance.

Peters, R. (1965) *Education as Initiation*, Inaugural Lecture, Institute of Education, University of London.

Rueschemeyer, D. (1983) Professional autonomy and the social control of expertise, in Dingwall, R. and Lewis, P. (eds) *The Sociology of the Professions: Lawyers, Doctors and Others*, London: Macmillan, pp. 38–58.

Sachs, J. (2003) *The Activist Teaching Professional*, Buckingham: Open University Press.

Times Educational Supplement (2008) 'Subject bodies struggling to attract members', 5 December.

Training and Development Agency (TDA) (n.d.) *Professional Teaching Standards*. Online, available at: www.tda.gov.uk/teachers/professionalstandards.aspx.

2 What makes a 'good' geography teacher?

John Morgan

The aims of this chapter are:

- to explore the models of the 'good' geography teacher found in text-books in geography education.
- to suggest that these models lack a realistic understanding of the political forces that shape the work of geography teachers in schools.
- to argue that there is a need to devise alternative models of the 'good' geography teacher.

There is no shortage of advice for teachers, new and experienced, about how to become a 'good' or 'better' teacher. Some informal 'research' in the Waterstones bookstore close to where I work revealed a wealth of titles, including the best-selling *How to Get the Buggers to. . .* series, the vaguely 'unprofessional' *How to Teach with a Hangover* and the slightly 'urban' *Pimp My Lesson*. Then there are more 'inspirational' texts such as *The 9 Habits of Highly Effective Teachers*. Less visible on the shelves are more 'serious' texts such as *Becoming a Teacher*, or *Learning to Teach in the Secondary School*. These are generic texts about teaching. On the whole they are interested in telling teachers what 'works' in real classrooms. Where research is used, it is assessed in terms of its potential to improve practice. Together, these texts seem to address the teacher as *competent craftsperson*, wherein, 'the teacher is configured and understood as one who "works upon" the raw material of their students, improving the extent and quality of learning and skills through the application and development of identified skills of their own' (Moore 2004: 4).

Whilst generic texts about teaching have their uses, teachers also look for more specific advice about how to teach their subject, and there is a long tradition of handbooks written for geography teachers, many of them by former teachers who are now involved in initial teacher education. Written with the benefit of hindsight and the luxury of being outside of the classroom, these texts are often strongly influenced by the model of teacher development that is dominant in university departments of education, namely the idea of the teacher as *reflective practitioner,* which places as much emphasis on teachers' own evaluations of their practice as on the planning and management skills into which these evaluations feed (see Chapter 3). These texts insist that teaching is a highly complex and contextual activity, where there are few sure-fire 'fixes' that can make life easier for teachers in classrooms, and that one's development as a teacher is dependent on the continual process of reflection-on-practice.

Such texts are sold as offering advice on how the reader can become a 'good' geography teacher, and are therefore useful sources of guidance as to what are the characteristics of the 'good' teacher. In the next part of this chapter, I undertake a reading of some of these texts in order to explore some of their ambiguities and tensions.

Self-help for geography teachers

In what follows, I want to discuss a sample of texts written for geography teachers which offer advice as to how to become a 'good' geography teacher.

The first text I want to consider is Leslie Jay's *Geography Teaching With a Little Latitude* (1981). Although this book was published as late as 1981, it has the feel of a 'museum-piece'. It has at its heart the dictionary definition of 'latitude' which includes a 'wide range', 'breadth in interpretation', 'freedom from restraint' and 'laxity'. This is the approach that Jay takes. He notes that nearly all the books that have been written about the teaching of geography concentrate on important, fundamental issues and are written in a serious vein, 'so serious, in fact, that many of those who teach or are preparing to teach never bother to read them' (1981: xi). The lessons they describe seem to be too good to be true and are therefore off-putting to the beginning teacher:

> Yet anyone who has observed an experienced teacher in action is impressed by the dexterity with which unexpected answers are treated, misunderstandings clarified, clumsy phrases re-worded and irrelevancies discarded. All of these verbal thrusts and parries are accompanied by supportive comments tailored to the individual pupil – a mild reproof here, a word of praise there, a gentle jest with another, creating a pattern of conversation which in a purposeful yet unforced manner advances the theme of the lesson without losing the attention or interest of the class.
>
> (1981: xi)

Geography Teaching with a Little Latitude sits at the cusp of two competing paradigms in geography teaching. The jokes, malapropisms and quizzes described in the book presume a charismatic teacher trying hard to inject 'a little judicious levity' into a subject burdened by the accumulation of facts and regional description. Teaching here is a performance, an act that requires high levels of verbal skill. But there is also an underlying sense of the changing nature of the relationships between teachers and students. The humour is that of the 'schoolboy' (and a grammar school one at that), but there is a serious point at stake, that of the quality of relationships between teachers and students. The final paragraph of Jay's book refers to how, in the 1970s, the teaching of geography had undergone a conceptual revolution, and this was likely to change the social relations of the classroom:

> Associated with the emergence of these new concepts and skills is a changed relationship between teacher and pupils, less formal than before, in which children are more vocal in expressing their opinions and preferences.
>
> (1981: 130)

The 'changed relationships' that Jay referred to offered new challenges to geography teachers, and by the time the book was published the model of the charismatic teacher enlivening geography lessons with anecdotes and humour was being replaced by a more systematic approach to the process of teaching and learning. Influenced by the educational sociology of the 1970s, teacher education became more concerned with close observation and analysis of the various elements of classroom practice. An example of this approach is found Frank Molyneaux and Harry Tolley's (1987) *Teaching Geography: a Teaching Skills Workbook*. The book was part of a series that grew out of a DES-financed Teacher Education Project which ran from 1976–80. The project explored general teaching skills: class management, questioning, explaining, and the handling of mixed-ability classes and exceptional pupils. The series was designed to 'examine basic teaching skills in their respective subject areas'. The context for this is important, as Trevor Kerry, the series editor, noted that there is mounting public pressure for increased accountability by the teaching profession: 'This series will, we believe, help to make teachers more analytical in their teaching and more articulate in expressing the rationale for their work' (1987: 5).

Teaching Geography: a Teaching Skills Workbook is divided into three sections: preparing to teach geography, teaching geography and reflections on geography teaching. The exercises focus in on classroom observation, recording and application, and readers are provided with a series of small scale exercises that allow them to analyse their classroom activity. In the final section of the book the authors return to the questions of accountability and evaluation, placing the onus firmly on the individual ('as a self-respecting professional you will wish always to be accountable to yourself'). Molyneaux and Tolley address the question of professionalism with reference to Hoyle's model of styles of professional behaviour. Hoyle distinguished between the 'restricted professional' teacher and the 'extended professional' teacher (1974: 13–19).

The 'restricted professional teacher' would be expected to:

- show a high level of classroom competence.
- reflect a child-centredness or sometimes a subject-centredness.
- possess a high degree of skill in understanding and handling children.
- derive high satisfaction from personal relationships with students.

- evaluate performance in terms of his or her own perceptions of changes in pupil behaviour and achievement.
- attend some short courses of a practical nature.

The 'extended professional teacher' would possess all of the above characteristics, but in addition:

- views work in the wider context of school, community and society.
- participates in a wide range of professional activities.
- is concerned to link theory and practice.
- is committed to some form of curriculum theory and mode of evaluation.

It is important to stress that the authors' focus on the question of professionalism for geography teachers was part of a broader concern about the status of teaching in the 1980s. They note that, since the 1970s, the increasing emphasis on accountability had led to a 'more contractual view of teaching by both employers and some employees'. They quote disapprovingly from a letter written by a teacher which expresses a 'contractual' view of teaching, suggesting that readers will 'no doubt find aspects of this view unacceptable'. They conclude that the twin concepts of accountability and evaluation 'must begin at the level of the individual practitioner' (1987: 74).

Teaching Geography: a Teaching Skills Workbook reflects in many ways some of the tensions that beset teacher education in the 1980s. David Hartley (2000) has described this period as one of 'doubt, reflection and reconstruction'. During this period, the 'grand narratives of psychology, sociology and philosophy began to give way to the niche narratives of the reflective practitioner'. The result was to claim that the greater validity and authenticity of expert teachers' routine, everyday knowledge could be represented and made real for the novice. The implicit and tacit knowledge generated by teachers whilst they were teaching could be rendered explicit and communicable. This was to be achieved through the process of reflection. The activities in *Teaching Geography: a Teaching Skills Workbook* are in line with this approach. The notion that there is a body of knowledge derived from disciplines is replaced by a focus on how individual student teachers experience their work. Thus, there is little attempt to provide a history of geographical education. Instead, students are asked to reflect on the geography they experienced in schools, comparing this to a colleague's experience. Another activity asked students to write a case history of their own geographical education up to the age of 18. The activities are designed for practical exploration and reflection in schools and classrooms, and the reader of this book is assured that the way to become a 'good' geography teacher is to observe, teach and reflect on their practice rather than follow recipes.

Hartley ponders the reasons why this shift towards a more individualistically based theory should occur. He notes that, within the social sciences, there was a tendency to favour 'agency'-based theories rather than 'structure'-

based theories, and that the 'reflective practitioner' emerged in that same consumerist age when we were all urged to reflect on our identities. The result, he suggests, is a growing polarisation between two kinds of knowledge: that generated in the academy (abstract, formal, propositional, generalisable, public and written) and that generated by teachers (contingent on time and place, practical, informal and anecdotal, either in written or oral form).

In many ways, Tony Fisher's *Developing as a Teacher of Geography* (1998) represents a 'sequel' to *Teaching Geography*. Published in 1998, it represents a text written in the light of developments in teacher training where courses were supposed to help beginning teachers to develop a series of 'professional competences'. At the heart of Fisher's book is an unresolved tension between the discourse of the 'reflective practitioner' and that of 'competence'. Early in the book, Fisher refers to the criticisms of the competence approach by Usher and Edwards:

> Discourses of competence attempt to repress certain conceptions of knowledge and understanding in order to sustain an agenda where competence-based qualifications appear to be the appropriate response. A regime of truth is established which derides certain forms of knowledge as 'theory', irrelevant to 'getting the job done well'.
>
> (1994: 115)

Usher and Edwards argue that discourses of competence threaten to colonise and dispel other views as to what counts as 'good' teaching:

> The competent teacher is constructed not as one who knows that something is the case, or knows how to teach, but who can actually teach competently according to pre-determined criteria of competences. The veiling of certain forms of knowledge as 'theory' to be removed from the curricula of teacher training is something that finds support among many trainee teachers, who thereby deny themselves the forms of autonomy and the right to be critical which were previously the defining characteristics of the teaching profession.
>
> (1994: 115)

This is perhaps the most worrying aspect of the discourse of competence. As more training takes place in schools which are seen to be the sites of 'real experience' rather than the 'out-of-touch' higher-education departments, the types of intellectual resources for understanding aspects of professional practice become unavailable. These would include a broader sense of the social aspects in which teaching takes place, an understanding of educational history and the existence of a variety of perspectives on teaching and learning, and more philosophical reflections on the nature of learning. As Usher and Edwards comment, teachers will still encounter problems, but are more likely to end up 'moaning in the staffroom' rather than mounting more considered responses.

Despite the threat of the competence discourse, Fisher seeks to hold on to the possibility that there is a space for autonomous and independent teachers. He asks, perhaps optimistically: 'Is the professionally competent, yet critically reflective, theorising, autonomous teacher too much to hope for?' (1998: 5). The book is based on the belief that

> the professional development which takes place in the early years of a teaching career is of fundamental importance, and that the beginning teacher who can function as a self-developing, autonomous professional will be best placed to gain the maximum benefit from these processes.
>
> (Fisher 1998: 1)

In many ways this is an inspiring and attractive agenda. However, there are some real contradictions in the approach offered. First, in order to become autonomous, a strong emphasis is placed on the role of collaboration, which relies on the existence of such collaborative communities of practice within schools. This is something that the book cannot assure, and indeed, at the time of its publication, changes were taking place in the nature of teachers' work which encouraged teachers to comply uncritically (i.e. teach to the test), challenged teachers' substantive identities, reduced the time teachers have to connect with, care for and attend to the needs of individual students, threatened teachers' sense of agency and resilience, and challenged teachers' capacities to maintain motivation, efficacy and thus, commitment (Day et al. 2007). Second, the nature of the text has the feel of a 'self-help' book. There are a series of exercises that encourage the beginning teacher to 'go deeper' into private aspects of the self rather than seek to understand the challenges they face using the more public discourses of politics and the social sciences. It might be argued that these would be more useful in helping teachers to maintain a realistic and more collaborative perspective on their work.

In summary, *Developing as a Teacher of Geography* can be read as reflective of a model of teacher development that, even as it was published, was struggling to maintain its position in the face of more 'practical' or 'pragmatic' views of what it means to teach geography. Indeed, it is significant that at this time Bill Marsden published *Geography 11–16: Rekindling Good Practice* (1996). With a sub-title like this, it is clear that the author thinks something has been lost.

Since this shift, publications directed at geography teachers have become increasingly geared towards more practical ways of coping with the demands of classrooms. Thus, the most significant text of recent years, David Lambert and David Balderstone's *Learning to Teach Geography in the Secondary School* (2000), now in its second edition (2010), is the product of a PGCE course that strives to meet the requirements of the Standards for QTS and still provide the basis for a version of extended professionalism. It is a weighty book, running to 479 pages, and this perhaps reflects the amount of material to be covered in the initial training year. One of its characteristics is its detailed description of practice, and, compared to Fisher's book, it offers much more of a 'course to be followed'. It is tempting to suggest that what characterises the 'good' geography teacher, in this version, is his or her ability to deal with more material, to recognise more complexity and to plan more exciting lessons. Graham Butt's *Reflective Teaching of Geography 11–18* (2002) covers much the same ground but is, if anything, more hidebound by the QTS 'Standards', and the notion of reflective practice is a much more functional one than that found in the texts of the 1980s. Thus:

> Effective reflection should be critical and set against established criteria or standards; it should involve target setting and be challenging without being unnecessarily threatening. The key element in good reflective practice is the ability to actually *change* aspects of one's teaching that are not up to standard. The impetus for this change should come from secure and impartial evidence, based on observation of current practice.
>
> (2002: 195)

This is a vaguely threatening definition of 'reflective practice', since it seems to imply that teaching is about the reflexive self-monitoring of one's performance against a set of standards that, presumably, have been decided elsewhere. If reflective practice is, as writers such as Fisher, Molyneaux and Tolley would imply, a matter of personal reflection in collaboration with colleagues, where does the notion of 'secure' and 'impartial' evidence come from?

This review of a sample of influential books written as sources of advice and guidance for geography teachers reveals some important features. In particular, there is a commitment to the discourse of the reflective practitioner despite the more recent moves towards more competence and pragmatic discourses. This commitment to a theoretical base in teacher education is hard to sustain in a situation where the emphasis is on the 'practical', and where more of a new teacher's initial training is 'delivered' in schools rather than in universities. It would be tempting to bemoan this situation and seek to 'rekindle' some earlier model of reflective practice (as is implied in Marsden's book). However, I think it is important to recognise that the situations in which schools and teachers find themselves in at the present time are very different, and that it is necessary to develop more relevant and appropriate models of teacher development. In particular, if we are concerned to restore a stronger sense of 'theory' to our work as geography teachers, we need to critically examine the type of theory that has underpinned ideas about the 'good' geography teacher. This is attempted in the following section.

Beyond the idealist legacy in geography teaching

It is a common complaint of beginning teachers that the ideas and approaches they encounter within university elements of initial teacher education seem far removed from their experiences of actual classrooms. Sometimes, upon arriving in schools, they are advised to 'ignore' what they are told in the university because schools are very different places, with a different set of demands. There is perhaps an element of truth in this, but in this section I want to suggest that rather than the problem being with 'theory' itself, it is in fact the type of 'theory' that is on offer that is the problem. In re-reading the books discussed in this chapter, it became clear that there is a certain type of 'theory' that is on offer to geography teachers. This can be characterised, following Kevin Harris (1992) in *Teachers: Constructing the Future,* as the 'idealist legacy'.

Harris suggests that many of the theories offered to teachers are based on 'idealism', which suggests that changes in our practices as teachers are best achieved through changing the way we think about our work as teachers. Harris identifies a number of problems with this 'theory'.

First, it assumes, either explicitly or implicitly, an atomistic stance to social relations. It lays out a context that displays teachers as free, autonomous, individual agents and it describes teacher practice within the terms of such a context. The good teacher is then able to influence individual pupils and bring about personal and education transformations. This ignores the complexity of the teacher–pupil relationships which are affected by relations of power and control.

Second, idealism in educational theory conflates concrete social institutions with abstract ideals. The most obvious example of this is the ways in which schooling and education are taken to be the same thing.

Third, idealism concentrates on notions such as 'democracy', 'equality' and 'personal autonomy', but less than critically it also suggests that the social formations to which the theory are meant to apply *are* actually democratic and egalitarian. The result is a conflict between the theory which guides practice and the actual outcomes of that practice.

Fourth, idealism exhorts moral and intellectual prescriptions which have a nice ring to them and read well as a projection of what things might be like in the best of all possible worlds. These sound nice, but their practical realisation requires the establishment of social conditions that could allow them to flourish. In the absence of these conditions, teachers are likely to feel that they are not living up to the high-minded ideas with which they entered the classroom.

In summary, the texts discussed in this chapter rely on idealist theories that stress the agency and autonomy of teachers in schools. As Harris notes, idealist theories can be comfortable in times of relative social stability and economic expansion, and especially for teachers in elite and privileged schools. These theories are ultimately unsatisfying because they do not speak to the lived experiences of teachers in schools. The result is that 'theory' gets a bad name, and that teachers are encouraged to seek out things that 'work' in classrooms. This literature, focused as it is on the individual geography teacher, does not address the wider contexts in which teachers work. In the next section, I suggest that there is a need to develop accounts of geography teaching that are more realistic in their understanding of the conditions under which geography teachers work.

The politics of teaching geography

What is striking about the experience of reading the texts written for geography teachers is that it would be hard to get a sense that the period in which they were written was one of profound changes in the nature of teachers' work. This is surprising since, as Stephen Ball argues:

> The politics of education since the early 1980s can be interpreted as centring upon a primary concern – the taming of teachers. The major thrust of much of the eruption of education policy during that period has been to control and discipline teachers.
>
> (2001: 10)

There is a vast literature that documents and seeks to explain the changing natures of teachers' work, and all that is offered here is a summary of some themes that illustrate the need to take seriously the wider political contexts in which geography teachers work. In his summary, Ball claims that there has been an increase in the technical elements of teachers' work and a reduction in the professional. For example, significant parts of teachers' practice are now codified in terms of attainment targets, programmes of study, teaching requirements, and measured in terms of national tests. Other examples include decisions about the reduction of the coursework elements in assessment and decisions that have effects on classroom organisation. In many schools, in response to the need to improve attainment, there is intense focus on the C/D borderline which effectively means that teachers have to choose to devote more time to some students rather than others. In all these cases, the space for professional and autonomous judgement is reduced.

There are important debates about the reasons for and extent of these changes in the nature of schooling. One of the most significant is that education is undergoing significant shifts in relation to the wider economy. For example, Gewirtz (2001) analyses the shift from an education system concerned with welfarist goals of social mobility and equal opportunities to the 'managerial school' focused on performance, image and accountability. This entails changes in our understanding of what and who schools are for, and consequences for what it means to be a pupil and a teacher within schools. She concludes that teachers are experiencing a loss of autonomy and an accelerated intensification of activity and stress; there is a decline in the sociability of teaching; and there is pressure on teachers to adopt more traditional pedagogies, with a focus on output rather than process.

Dissertation summary

Oldroyd, Amy (2003) 'The Key Stage 3 Strategy – is it Good Geography?'

These developments have had significant impacts on what it means to be a geography teacher in schools, but they are nowhere to be found in the texts produced for geography teachers, which still tend to be set within an idealist framework. However, many of these developments are evident in Amy Oldroyd's Masters' dissertation on the MA course in Geography Education at the Institute of Education, which explored the question: 'The key Stage 3 Strategy – is it good geography?' This was a study of the impact of the National Strategy within her own geography department, focusing on planning, assessment, departmental action planning, teacher development and Key Stage 3 results. She collected and analysed documentation, interviewed members of the geography department and the Key Stage 3 strategy leader, and did a self-reflective analysis.

Clearly, the department described by Oldroyd performed well in terms of Ofsted's criteria. Yet Oldroyd provides evidence to suggest that the strategy had influenced the work of the department in a variety of ways. Examples include: planning, where in schemes of work a section on geographical skills was replaced by 'citizenship skills'; the adoption of the geography department of a 'four-part lesson', so that lesson plans 'follow a strategy structure, rather than a specifically geographical one, raising opportunities for development of literacy and numeracy skills, but completely omitting any specific mention for the development of the geography' (2003: 62); action planning where the language of the Key Stage 3 strategy: ('Assessment for learning', 'Intervention toolkit', 'Writing across the curriculum', 'Leading Learning') dominated the plans written for the geography department; and teacher development, where prior to May 2002, 75 per cent of the training received by members of the geography department was directly related to the subject. Post-strategy introduction, however, only 12 per cent of training has been geography-specific.

Oldroyd asks the question of whether, instead of being geographers and good geography teachers, members of the department are to become merely good Strategy strand teachers or good literacy and numeracy teachers? An interview with the Strategy manager revealed the benefits of this approach to the Senior Leadership team. From a more critical perspective, given that teachers have been required to change their practices with little consultation, it might be argued that the Senior Leadership team has been able to exercise more control and power over teachers' work. Whilst the teachers Oldroyd interviewed recognised some benefits, they doubted that they had led to the teaching of 'good' geography.

Oldroyd's account is a useful case study of some of the ways in which geography teachers have lost control of the curriculum. The idealism that is found in much of the literature provided for geography teachers has not helped to nurture and sustain teachers in the face of a determined *realpolitik* that seeks to redefine the nature of teachers' work. Previously important aspects of widely accepted 'good' practice in the geography department have been undermined by the KS3 Strategy. The four-part lesson conflicts with the process of enquiry, the focus on limited versions of literacy and numeracy crowd out important geographical skills, lessons become more geared to meeting the pedagogical needs of the Strategy than valid and meaningful geographical content, and the drive to create integrated Foundation-stage subjects undermines subject distinctiveness.

So far, this has been a rather depressing story. I have suggested that the strong tendencies of idealism in accounts of geography teaching have meant that there is a strong suspicion of theory and that geography teachers' work has been significantly altered by moves to control and redefine classroom practice. Geography teachers have been unable to challenge this. Indeed, where Oldroyd's analysis is weakest is in terms of its ability to answer the question of what 'good' geography is. As one of the teachers Oldroyd interviewed commented, 'I've never really known what it's like to teach geography without the KS3 Strategy.'

Ways forward

Oldroyd's research into the geography taught in her school raises a very interesting dilemma: this is a successful geography department, it satisfies the school's programme for improvement, it is praised by Ofsted, yet the geographers in the department are clearly worried that this may be at the expense of 'good' geography! In many ways this reflects current thinking in educational policy and is expressed clearly in a document published by the DCSF called *Smoking Out Underachievement: Guidance and Advice to Help Secondary Schools Use Value Added Approaches with Data*. The guidance is intended to help schools make sense of the data that is provided to them about pupils' performance. It is intended to allow teachers to identify the learning needs of each individual pupil, understand how far each pupil is hitting the required target and to identify the school's strength and weaknesses. The data will be used to ask questions about how the school is performing. Thus governors can ask how do the school's standards compare with national standards? Headteachers can ask which are the strong/weak departments? And who are the strong/weak teachers? Teachers can ask is progress good enough? The emphasis is all on the measurement of performance, with governors, headteachers, subject leaders and classroom teachers all called upon to assess and measure pupils' attainment and ask questions about whether that performance is coming up to standard.

In this situation, I would argue that the one thing that teachers will not be asked to do is think carefully about the nature of their subject. Instead, the focus in on measuring children's attainment and monitoring their performance against specific 'outcomes'. The question remains: is this good geography? To answer this question, teachers may have to look outside of the limited and limiting frames set by Headteachers and Senior Leaders. For example, consider the following statement from Alistair Bonnett's *What is Geography?*:

Good geography, a geography able to explore, connect, map, and engage, requires freedom. Yet freedom is easily lost. The society of long-work hours, constant surveillance and materialist, isolated lives, is a society in which freedom is dying and with it the large horizons and outward disposition of geography. One of the most tragic aspects of this enclosing state of comfortable passivity is how it affects children. Increasingly, children are deprived of the freedom to explore, to roam and hide away out of the reach of adults. The traffic and 'stranger danger' mean that streets are too risky, so too the parks. And what really is the point of unsupervised play?

In a culture where children are expected to be always visible, to be meeting 'targets' and achieving 'outcomes', this question becomes harder to answer. Both work and play are now scripted as useful and productive 'opportunities'. For freedom and adventure read 'supervised outdoor learning experience' and 'professionally designed educational trip'. Children soon find that their only 'downtime', the only place where they are not being appraised, is when they are sat in front of a console or TV. In depriving children – and adults too – of environments in which they are free to explore and where risks can be taken, we are creating the conditions for the hollowing out of the geographical imagination.

(2008: 99–100)

The society of long-hours, constant surveillance, materialism and isolation that Bonnett describes is one where economic policies have led to the dominance of the market in all aspects of our lives. It is this logic that gives rise to 'performance management', school 'league tables' and 'personalized learning', and it may be that recovering a 'good' geography, one that provides children with the opportunities to explore, connect, map and engage, will require us to work to come up with alternative definitions and practices in schools.

For discussion

- What does it mean to be a good teacher in your school or geography department? Who decides?
- Imagine your geography department has recently appointed a recently qualified geography teacher. What support could you offer that is realistic in that it avoids the dangers of idealism?
- In 1973, Douglas Holly warned about the problem of teachers 'teaching to the test' as a case of 'professional cheating'. Now that teaching to the test is practised on a mass scale, how can geography teachers maintain their belief in what they believe is 'good' geography?

Further reading

1 Lambert, D. and Balderstone, D. (2000) *Learning to Teach Geography in the Secondary School* (RoutledgeFalmer). This book is widely regarded as the 'market-leader' in

introductory texts for new geography teachers, so perhaps provides one answer to the question of what makes a good geography teacher.

2 Moore, A. (2004) *The Good Teacher* (RoutledgeFalmer). Moore provides an interesting account of the changing discourses on 'good' teaching, and goes into more detail about the issues discussed in this chapter.

3 Usher, R. and Edwards, R. (1994) *Postmodernism and Education* (Routledge). This book still provides a useful and challenging account of the role of education in the contemporary world.

References

Ball, S. (2001) 'Better read: theorizing the teacher!', in J. Dillon and M. Maguire (eds) *Becoming a Teacher: Issues in Secondary Teaching*. Buckingham: Open University Press, pp. 10–22.

Bonnett, A. (2008) *What is Geography?* London: Sage.

Butt, G. (2002) *Reflective Teaching of Geography 11–18*. London: Continuum.

Day, C., Sammons, P., Stobart, G., Kington, A. and Qing Gu (2007) *Teachers Matter: Connecting Lives, Work and Effectiveness*. Buckingham: Open University Press.

DfES (2004) *Smoking Out Underachievement: Guidance and Advice to Help Secondary Schools Use Value Added Approaches with Data*. London: DfES.

Gewirtz, S. (2001) *The Managerial School: Post-welfarism and Social Justice in Education*. London: Routledge.

Fisher, T. (1998) *Developing as a Teacher of Geography*. Cambridge: Chris Kington Publishing.

Harris, K. (1992) *Teachers: Constructing the Future*. London: The Falmer Press.

Hartley, D. (2000) 'Shoring up the pillars of modernity: teacher education and the quest for certainty', *International Studies in Sociology of Education* 10(2): 113–31.

Holly, D. (1973) *Beyond Curriculum: Changing Secondary Education*. London: Hart-Davis, MacGibbon.

Hoyle, E. (1974) 'Professionality, professionalism and control in teaching', *London Education Review* 3(2): 13–19.

Jay, L. (1981) *Geography Teaching with a Little Latitude*. London: George Allen and Unwin.

Kerry, T. (1987) 'Editor's preface', in F. Molyneaux and H. Tolley, *Teaching Geography: a Teaching Skills Workbook*. Basingstoke: Macmillan Education, p. 5.

Lambert, D. and Balderstone, D. (2000) *Learning to Teach Geography in the Secondary School*. London: RoutledgeFalmer.

Marsden, W. (1996) *Geography 11–16: Rekindling Good Practice*. London: David Fulton.

Moore, A. (2004) *The Good Teacher*. London: RoutledgeFalmer.

Molyneaux, F. and Tolley, H. (1987) *Teaching Geography: a Teaching Skills Workbook*. Basingstoke: Macmillan Education.

Oldroyd, A. (2003) 'The Key Stage 3 Strategy – is it good geography?' Unpublished Masters Dissertation, University of London, Institute of Education.

Usher, R. and Edwards, R. (1994) *Postmodernism and Education*. London: Routledge.

3 Reflecting critically on practice

Sheila King

The aims of this chapter are:

- to explore the much used term 'reflective practice'.
- to understand how the process of critical reflection links theory and practice.
- to consider how teachers can develop their skills in reflective practice to benefit planning and teaching.

Since this chapter is linked to Toh's (2004) MA dissertation, it is fitting to begin with her observation about the relationship between experience and meaning. Conventional wisdom suggests that people learn from their mistakes, but Toh notes that it is easy to pass from one situation to the next, missing the opportunity to learn from those experiences. So it is for many of us teaching in educational settings all across the globe. Classrooms and other learning environments are such complex places that unravelling the intricacies of what goes on is a difficult task. This chapter proposes that critical reflection on practice must be an integral part of any teacher's work because it equips them to deal with the varied issues, encounters and contexts in which they will teach. It supports teachers in being adaptive and reactive to changes in time.

Of course all teachers review and reflect. Much of this is done on the bus going home or awaiting sleep in bed, and so is 'solitary in the head, unstructured reflection' (Moore 2004: 110). Such reflection frequently focuses on negative experiences and short-term solutions to immediate issues. By comparison, reflective practice goes beyond any common-sense approach. It is a deeper and constructive process which encourages both inexperienced and experienced professionals to reflect explicitly and critically so that practice is improved. By engaging in this process, the teachers' own theories towards pedagogy are given value and teachers take greater ownership of their professional and learning processes rather than relying on the 'good teaching' of universities, consultants and research centres (Zeichner 1994: 10).

The rest of this chapter deals with the way in which reflective practice is used by policy-makers, teacher educators and teachers to improve their work and ultimately to improve the learning of their pupils. Before this and to set some context I will consider one other model of the teacher which sits somewhat uncomfortably at times alongside the reflective practitioner: that of the competent practitioner.

The competent practitioner model

Initial teacher training in England exists in a statutory framework in which there are a number of Standards that student teachers need to achieve in order to be recommended for Qualified Teacher Status. This competency model of training began in 1992 and the frequency with which revisions through government circulars have been issued since then indicates the interest government at the time had in teacher training: Circulars 9/92 (DFE 1992), 14/93 (DFE 1993), 10/97 (DfEE 1997), 4/98 (DfEE 1998), DfES and TTA (2002) and TDA (2007). A competency model of teacher *training* rather than the notion of teacher *education* preferred by universities became established, and full details of this model and the process of its inception and revisions can be found in Butt (2002), Moore (2000) and Heilbronn (2008).

Since 1992, largely as a result of these government directives, teacher training has become more focused on the practicalities of learning and teaching and less on the theory. This was strongly influenced by the directive that 24 weeks of a secondary PGCE student's time and 18 weeks of a primary teacher's time was to be school-based. Another influential development was that the high-status Ofsted inspection system for England, which ultimately determines the number of training places and therefore the funding an institution receives, became strongly influenced by the competency model of training (Ofsted/TTA 1996). In consequence, and driven by the necessity to achieve high grades from Ofsted inspections of initial teacher training, universities and the alternative school-based training routes tend to have adopted the competency model. In practice this meant the development of a 'tick-box' mentality where student teachers gather evidence against each Standard. Evidence collected to demonstrate a teacher's ability to teach can became fragmented into compartmentalised segments. There were many critics. Hagger and McIntyre (2006: 63) state: 'nobody could seriously argue that learning to meet each of the standards separately could be equated with learning to teach.' Moore (2000: 126) argues that one difficulty of the competency model is that the competencies are seen to provide the entire syllabus and so suggest that the ingredients of 'good teaching' can be itemised. This implies that by mastering these segments anyone can make an effective teacher, without any sense of their holistic practice. He also highlights the lack of exploration of 'what makes an *effective* teacher' and, he argues, the competency model attempts to define a universally 'good' teacher without reference to personal differences and contextual backgrounds. Another critic, Bernstein (1996: 6), suggests a more political agenda with blame for any educational failure conveniently moved to the individual teacher and school rather than the more complex issues of the educational process within an increasingly complex educational system and society.

The reflective practitioner model

At the same time as the competent practitioner model was being developed, the parallel model of the reflective practitioner was also adopted by many teacher educators and the picture remains broadly the same at the time of writing. Scrutiny of prospectuses and course handbooks for many initial teacher education programmes and professional development courses highlight their aim to produce reflective professionals. Many journal articles, books and conference titles include the term 'reflective' and its derivatives.

The reflective-practitioner model goes beyond the acquisition of competencies or skills required for successful teaching, but encourages the teacher to 'reflect constructively upon ongoing experience as a way of developing those skills and knowledge and improving the quality and effectiveness of one's work' (Moore 2000: 128). One of the key words here is 'constructively'. Most teachers at some time have tossed and turned in the small hours of the morning over what to do with class 6A or a particular pupil for whom no strategy seems to work. Other teachers may 'coast' as their university tutors, NQT mentors or school managers are no longer there to challenge their work and they develop too low expectations of their pupils. Without a mental process to consider improvements, this is not true reflective practice. Even where there is a will and even when the experience and wisdom of other teacher educators can be utilised, it is ultimately up to the teachers themselves to be 'sufficiently aware of what they are doing in their teaching for them to be able to subject their developing or established practices to anything like the necessary degree of regular critical scrutiny' (Hagger and McIntyre 2006: 56).

The development of the reflective practice model

Most, if not all, new teachers could attempt an explanation of the term 'reflective practice' but I remain sceptical that, despite the rhetoric, the concept is well understood. I suspect many teachers groan at the mention of the words 'reflective practice', chiefly because at worst it is used for little more than 'thinking about' or 'evaluating', and without clear purpose and informed thinking the process is of little use.

There is a very large literature on reflective practice which is increasingly common to health, the law and other professions. The 'modern' father of reflective practice is often said to be Dewey (1933, 1938). Dewey identified two parts to practice: the *process* of how decisions are made and the *content and experience* which is the substance that drives the thinking. Schön applied

Dewey's work to the teaching profession (Schön 1987; 1991) and argued that:

> [the reflective practitioner] can surface and criticise the tacit understandings that have grown up around the repetitive experiences of a specialised practice, and can make new sense of the situations of uncertainty or uniqueness which he may allow himself to experience.
>
> (Schön 1991: 61)

Schön understood the complexities of teaching contexts, describing them as 'swampy lowlands where situations are confusing 'messes' incapable of technical solutions' (1991: 42) and where teachers become complacent and experience inertia because the complexities are too great to make sense of.

If readers of this chapter wish to avail themselves of more literature on reflective practice, then Zeichner (1994), Moon (2004), Moore (2004) and, in a geographical context, Butt (2002) are useful starting points. There are critics of reflective practice too (Eraut 1994). One criticism is that the practice is too introspective to benefit the wider profession, but dialogues between professionals and the development of learning sets and communities of practice can mitigate this issue. Many student teachers, especially in subject areas where writing (in a reflective/analytical way) does not always come easily, complain of the endless written accounts that training courses in reflective practice can demand. This can and should be overcome by a strong element of discussion, problem-solving and peer-coaching techniques.

Critical reflection

Critical reflection is the basis of reflective practice and involves an individual analysing, reconsidering and questioning professional and personal experience. The critical aspect comes in adding depth and breadth to the meanings of these experiences by asking deeper questions. It further requires the reflector to be open-minded to the validity of others' perspectives and crucially to the context in which the activity takes place.

> Perhaps even more central to adult learning than elaborating established meaning schemes is the process of reflecting back on prior learning to determine whether what we have learned is justified under present circumstances. This is a crucial learning process egregiously ignored by learning theorists.
>
> (Mezirow 1990: 5)

In the real world, critical reflection may just as likely lead to self-justification, self-indulgence or self-pity. It may also lead to disillusionment as reflective practitioners unsupported by their institutions in finding ways to change, feel frustrated. Mezirow (1990) suggests critical reflection is transformational, but this is likely to be so only if teachers practise this in a supportive school culture or higher-education environment.

When individuals acknowledge their personal context, bias and prejudices, their life history or autobiography, the term 'reflexive practice' is used (Moore 2000; Leat 1997). Moore (2000) claims reflexive practice moves reflective practice away from the concept of the teacher as the rational, unified self, somehow removed from the social circumstances in which he or she is constructed, towards a notion that 'self' is constructed, many-faceted and continuously developing. It involves the meta-level: how the teacher reflects on the *ways* they reflect. In many geography classrooms where 'Thinking Skills' activities are used (Leat 1998; Nichols and Leat 2001), pupils reach higher levels of understanding when they engage in *how* their thinking led to their conclusions and this is equally necessary for reflexive practice.

Developing critically reflective practice

New teachers often reach a crucial step in their learning when the classrooms that they thought they knew become increasingly complex places. Table 3.1 illustrates four teachers' thoughts after they had engaged in a period of critical reflection. In the following, more detailed example, Sophie, a student teacher, was observing an experienced teacher's classroom during the initial weeks of her course and writing up her reflections.

Initially she wrote:

> I think the most important feature of the class was how strong the unit seemed.... energy seemed to have been harnessed by encouraging the students to be independent learners, by allowing them freedom to move around, to use resources on the walls or to start up the computer.... Using an understanding of the ecosystem model[1] it is clear that one of the most important aspects of this class is its history of long established practices and routine.

Of the framework used to structure the observation Sophie wrote: '[it] helps to direct and guide observation, breaking down complexities that are too unmanageable to be dealt with initially as a whole.'

Later she concluded: 'I do think that I have improved [in classroom observation] and certainly the use of the ecosystem model has helped to guide my observation. Slowly the classroom is becoming a little less familiar' (Lambert and Sankey 1994: 175–181).

Sophie's interesting, final phrase surely signals a geography PGCE student making progress on her learning journey.

More-experienced teachers also benefit from having their accepted understanding of their pupils, teaching and classrooms challenged. However, this is more difficult once mentors for initial teacher training and the induction year no longer have a role to play and staff development is largely dependent on

Table 3.1 Extracts from PGCE assignments

'I have enjoyed reflecting on the big concepts and processes that school geography aims to develop in students. This is particularly important at this time when geography as a subject is under threat.'

'Learning to work within this reflective practice model in the two schools where I have worked has changed the way I view teaching. I understand teaching has a strong craft component but is chiefly characterised by ongoing self reflection, collaboration, adaptation and learning.'

'I have developed my reflective strategies and moved – to some extent at least – past ritualistic reflection towards more authentic and constructive self reflection.'

'It hasn't been easy to process some of the powerful emotions I felt when things went disastrously wrong and to turn them into constructive experiences. It's been hard to act on advice when I sometimes didn't want to ... but it almost always worked.'

the school's leadership team. Therefore it is up to individual teachers to provide time and mechanisms for evaluating their work, with occasional views provided by pupils, other external mentors, coaches and inspectors.

A teacher's critical reflection leads to more than just a gain in knowledge; it should also challenge the concepts and theories by which sense is made of that knowledge. The observer sees not just more, but differently, and it is usually true that sharing the process with a peer or mentor/coach leads to an even deeper level of understanding. The final stage of reflection is action, with the teacher's self-review and reflection cycle beginning all over again.

How does critical reflection link theory and practice?

Reflective practice must be learnt rather than taught, and it requires the teacher to have an open mind which is predicated on improvement through practice and informed by theory. Here is another difficult term. What is 'theory'? At its simplest level, theory may guide you in what you do or don't do (see also Chapter 11). A teacher who has a framework of behaviour in his or her head for when greeting a class or marking a piece of homework is using theory. Learning theories have two main values, according to Hill (2002). One is in providing us with vocabulary and a conceptual framework for interpreting the learning that we observe. The other is in suggesting where to look for solutions to practical problems. The theories do not give us solutions, but they do direct our attention to those variables that are crucial in finding solutions. It is unlikely that teachers whose practice is largely uninformed by the theories of others will develop the professional competence required by teachers in the twenty-first century.

The linking of theory and practice becomes a tension in teacher education when theory is seen by teachers as the domain of the universities and detached from schools; when it is 'seen as an extension of the theoretical perspectives of the universities into schools clearly distinguished from the student teachers' everyday work there' (Hagger and McIntyre 2006: 60). However, there are signs that in an increasing number of schools these boundaries are breaking down. One key factor is that dedicated senior school mentors coordinate initial and continuing professional development and as such are professional, school-based educators. Teachers are more frequently engaging in funded and non-funded practitioner and action research. PGCE courses work more and more in partnership with schools in delivering professional development; constructing research projects of interest to both schools and universities. Three examples illustrate how theory is increasingly being constructed with practitioners:

1   Eight excellent practitioners in schools facing challenging circumstances and which have been identified as having excellent practice in initial teacher education and/or induction are working with university staff to identify barriers to teacher development and ways these schools have overcome the barriers.
2   Five schools are evaluating a project designed jointly by university tutors and school staff in which student teachers act as teaching assistants to prepare them for their future role in working with teaching assistants.
3   Teachers in five schools alongside three university tutors are defining the benefits engagement in ITE brings to schools.

Examples of the outcomes of many other teacher research projects can be found at the Teacher Training Resource Bank (www.ttrb.ac.uk), and at the Department for Children, Schools and Families (www.standards.dfes.gov.uk/ntrp).

One of the tensions faced particularly during initial teacher training and the induction year by teachers who engage in critical reflection is a fear that if they question the work of their subject departments and schools in an open and honest way this may not be interpreted well by some schools. It is a fine balance to establish an effective dialogue without being seen as confrontational. However, school leaders and managers increasingly see their schools as learning communities and take professional development more seriously.

In the following section I wish to suggest some practical strategies that encourage critical reflection. These focus on the exploration of the personal viewpoints and autobiographies that shape our approach to teaching, and so enable reflexivity. Some ideas and examples are more appropriate to novice or recently qualified teachers, while others may be preferred by experienced teachers or teachers engaging in specific enquiries and research.

Questions as a starting point

The identification of 'good' quality questions raised by teachers will support critical evaluation. Roth (1989) includes some of the behaviours and processes that build well-grounded reflection, and these appear in brackets alongside the questions below. Such questions might be:

*   What did pupil X leave the lesson knowing that he did not 'know' before he entered? (Would the pupil give the same answer?) (*Questioning the basis of what is done.*)
*   Was the way I chose to teach episode Y as successful as with previous classes? Should I use a problem-solving approach again? (*Asking 'what if'... seeking alternatives.*)
*   How will I judge if greater learning has been achieved through the group activity than had the exercise been done independently? (*Exploring alternatives.*)
*   Were all pupils engaged in the task? If not, what were they doing when off-task? Would my teaching assistant say the same? (*Asking for others' viewpoints.*)

Specific to geography teachers is the notion of teaching and learning 'good geography', by which is meant 'accurate, meaningful, up-to-date and access-ible' geography (Butt 2002: 196). This can be challenging in a subject where many teachers are non-specialists or have senior responsibilities so may not find it so easy to keep up-to-date. High-order questions that are geography specific might include:

*   Did the use of the glacier animations really improve understanding? How do I know this? (*Keeping an open mind.*)
*   Did the thinking-skills 'mystery' on local planning develop conceptual development rather than being simply a fun activity? (*Synthesising and testing.*)
*   Does my use of Barnaby Bear with Year 3 improve pupils' geographical understanding? (*Considering consequences.*)
*   In what ways did my unit on 'Trade not Aid' provide extended oppor-tunities for the significant number of very able pupils in my class? (*Seeking underlying rationale.*)

Frameworks for observation

It is generally accepted that learning through reflection is more potent if the observation process is structured and based on a framework to guide the act of reflection. While this chapter does not describe any specific frameworks, they are widely available (see for example Wragg 1994, and for geography specific examples, Lambert and Balderstone 2000: 414–419; King 2000). However, rather than choosing 'off-the-peg' frameworks designed by others, observers should build their own for specific purposes. In themselves, obser-vations can be illuminating, but it is the opportunity to discuss the observa-tions with the observed teacher or a peer that will probably add most value to the task. Jointly decided and pre-determined questions may form a useful base for building such a framework for this discussion.

Diaries and journals as a record of reflection

One technique used to capture reflections is the keeping of a diary or journal, originally in written form but increasingly as video diaries. This enables the 'invisible to be rendered visible' and a dialogue, often with oneself, about practice to be set up (Moore 2000: 129). Such dialogue encourages taken-for-granted assumptions and practices to be questioned, and for alternative approaches to classroom practice to be tried out and debated. In keeping a written record of their reflection, writers are encouraged to be frank and honest, as it is from this that important insights are more likely to arise. In addition, writers are encouraged to express themselves freely without need to observe the normal academic practices involved in writing.

One challenge to reflective practitioners is to move away from description to a deeper level of analysis. In a small study of 20 PGCE student teachers' 1000-word reflections, it became clear that the quality of their reflections improved towards the end of the course. Many initial statements began 'I have', I did', 'I was able to', 'I participated in and enjoyed' and 'I made more sense of' but they remained descriptive. One teacher who had a more developed approach wrote:

> In the beginning I thought I could 'just do it' like Mr White. I just didn't realise that what I saw was the tip of the iceberg and he'd been learning their names since term started, he knew his classroom and resources and he could *anticipate* some things that might go wrong. My early observations just didn't get to that level of depth and I was really keen to keep observing after I'd taken over my classes as I felt I learned more from having the deeper understanding.
>
> (Personal reflection 2008)

Conclusions in themselves are not the key outcome of reflective practice and should be reserved for the final stage of any writing logs since early conclusions may inhibit further insights and solutions. The keeping of reflective journals will not appeal to all teachers' learning styles and the ability to write in an appropriate way needs to be learnt as much as any other technique. However, the experience can be invaluable as one teacher wrote, 'I learnt the ability to constantly reflect on my practice and continue to make small changes that resulted in a cycle of improvement' (Personal reflection).

Critical 'friends'

The term critical 'friend' is used here to describe a colleague who may or may not have the role of mentor, coach or line manager. At best it will be someone whose judgement and decisions the teacher trusts. Their role is to enter into a meaningful discussion about the reflections, whether they are based on observed lessons or written accounts, and they should challenge and provide feedback in a supportive manner.

There is no doubt that an effective mentor in the initial year(s) of teaching can do much to establish a new *reflective* practitioner. For example, Mark wrote:

> my NQT mentor really challenged my work with the sixth form. She said I didn't use the same humour or fun activities that I utilised well in Key Stages 3 and 4 ... and she was right! It was a really challenging dialogue we developed.
>
> (Personal reflection 2008)

One student teacher at the start of her career described a similar experience where she was strongly affected by the senior mentor who described many of the pupils' difficult home lives; something the student teacher had not encountered in her own schooling: 'I found teaching in that school unsettling and emotionally upsetting at first but it became fantastically rewarding, especially with the help and advice from the other teachers' (Personal reflection).

Within the last decade, the mentor model of teacher development has become more influenced by a coaching approach and this is well documented (Pask and Joy 2007; Robertson 2005; Fogarty and Pete 2007). The employment of more in-house school coaches, the rise in popularity of professional development coaching courses in education and the intended introduction of school-based coaches as a key part of the government's new national Master of Teaching and Learning all support this (TDA 2008). What this brings to the reflective-practitioner model is a richness of questioning, listening and thinking; a model that encourages different levels of thinking and participants to continue their reflections at home or a few days/weeks later.

The problem with reflective practice

Outcomes of reflection are frequently hard to define and quantify. They often involve the ability of the teacher to communicate, present, analyse and interact. A reflective practitioner's success is judged not through the numbers of pupils passing tests, important though that is, but on the nature of the learning process informed within the context in which it takes place. The 'messy complexity of the classroom' and the likelihood that we will never fully understand our practice are acknowledged (Goodson and Walker 1991: xii). Teachers also teach with a combination of outcomes in mind and these may be short term (within a lesson) or longer term (by the end of a unit of work) and focused on cognitive (intellectual) or affective (social, emotional or attitudinal) aspects of learning (Kyriacou 1997: 8). In addition, teachers personalise their teaching so that their response to a pupil with a learning difficulty may be different to those of a very-able pupil. So reflection is a complex activity and one which is strongly contextualised to the learning situation(s). The revised Standards for Qualified Teacher Status (TDA 2007) now recognise the value of critical reflection and state that teachers should be able to:

Standard Q7   Reflect on and improve their practice.
Standard Q8   Have a creative and constructively critical approach toward innovation.
Standard Q29   Evaluate the impact of their teaching on the progress of all learners and modify their planning and classroom practice where necessary.

However, this is a small step. High-quality reflective practice encourages teachers to take risks and make changes without fear of failure.

Dissertation summary

Elaine Toh (2004) 'Understanding Reflective Practice in Geography: Teachers' Views, its Role and Feasibility – "Implications for Professional Development"'

Toh's dissertation focuses on the process of undertaking reflective practice on geography teachers in Singapore. Inspired by the power of reflective practice on her own development, Toh wanted to explore how teachers responded to reflecting on their practice, and the problems they encountered.

Toh's literature review traces the development of the idea of reflective practice, and explores how key thinkers (like Dewey and Schön) have adapted and developed the concept. In her literature review, Toh identifies stages of reflective practice and strategies that teachers can use to develop it. From this extensive body of literature, Toh identifies which strategies and techniques will fit in with her research focus – that of getting teachers to engage with thinking reflectively.

Toh's research design was very ambitious and experimental. Building on the review of relevant literature, she developed a series of Self-Reflection Sheets, and recruited a number of geography teachers in Singapore who agreed to fill these sheets in every two weeks (along with a pre- and post-research questionnaire). So she could monitor the data collection, all the teachers agreed to email the Self-Reflection Sheets directly to her. However, it became clear as the research progressed that, despite having followed all the conventions about negotiating access, some of Toh's teachers found it very difficult to fill in the sheets as often as she requested. It was at this stage that Toh had to be flexible in her research design. Her results started to illuminate unexpected phenomena.

In her results and discussion, Toh analyses the questionnaires she received, and her communications with the participants. Toh identifies that the process of engaging with critical reflection was very challenging and time-consuming for the teachers involved. In her conclusion, she reviews ways that the research design could have been adapted, but also highlights some valuable observations: that the process of reflection and thinking deeply about one's practice has the potential to transform practice, but that this process requires a great deal of commitment and support. In true reflective style, Toh also identifies how the process of research itself can have a positive impact on both the researcher and the participants in the research.

For discussion

- In what ways has your practice been critically reflective to date? Can you think of any key moments that have made you think differently about teaching?
- Consider the tasks you have been asked to do on professional development courses (including your initial teacher education). Were these designed to make you critically reflective, or competent? Which had the most impact on you?
- What do you want to improve in your practice now? What questions could help you to achieve that?

Further reading

1 Butt, G. (2002) *Reflective Teaching of Geography 11–18*. London and New York: Continuum. This book is part of a series on reflective teaching as applied to subject areas; in this case, geography. You will not find discussion or debate on the areas included in this chapter but rather it is highlighted here as a book which enables practitioners to apply theory and research relating to reflective practice to their own work.
2 Heibronn, R. (2008) *Teacher Education and the Development of Practical Judgement*. London: Continuum. This book covers the history and context of teacher training and education in England, the teacher as reflective practitioner and the nature of teacher knowledge and understanding together. It considers the roles that teacher experience, mentors and research play in developing that reflective practice.
3 Kyriacou, C. (1997) *Effective Teaching in Schools: Theory and Practice*. London: Nelson Thornes. *Effective Teaching in Schools* is an accessible, general book which defines high-quality classroom practice. The book helps to develop the essential skills of reflective practice, yet remains strongly practical so it becomes an effective bridge between the theory students need to put their experience in context and the practice which allows them to build on theoretical work where it matters in the classroom.

Note

1 The ecosystem framework for observing classrooms is a useful model based on the concept of an ecosystem as a way of relating the multitude of parts within a classroom to a view of the whole. It is argued that terms such a 'fragile', 'balance',

'dynamic change' and 'interdependence' are relevant to both forest and classroom settings. The model is too complex to be discussed in this chapter, but full details are in Lambert and Sankey (1994: 175–181) or summarised in King (2000: 20–23).

References

Bernstein, B. (1996) *Pedagogy, Symbolic Control and Identity*. London: Taylor and Francis.

Butt, G. (2002) *Reflective Teaching of Geography 11–18*. London and New York: Continuum.

Dewey, J. (1933) *How We Think*. New York: Prometheus Books.

Dewey, J. (1938) *Experience and Education*. New York: Collier Macmillan.

DFE (1992) *Initial Teacher Training*. Circular 9/92, London: HMSO.

DFE (1993) *Initial Teacher Training*. Circular 14/93, London: HMSO.

DfEE (1997) *Teaching: High Status, High Standards, Requirements for Courses of Initial Teacher Training*. Circular 10/97, London: DfEE.

DfEE (1998) *Teaching: High Status, High Standards, Requirements for Courses of Initial Teacher Training*. Circular 4/98, London: DfEE.

DfES and TTA (2002) *Qualifying to Teach: Professional Standards for Qualified Teacher Status and Requirements for Initial Teacher Training*. London: DfES.

Eraut, M. (1994) *Developing Professional Knowledge and Competence*. Sussex: Falmer Press.

Fogarty, R. and Pete, B. (2007) *From Staff Room to Classroom: a Guide for Planning and Coaching Professional Development*. California: Corwin Press.

Goodson, I. and Walker, R. (1991) *Biography, Identity, and Schooling: Episodes in Educational Research*. London: Falmer Press.

Hagger, H. and McIntyre, D. (2006) *Learning Teaching from Teachers: Realising the Potential of School-based Teacher Education*. Oxford: Open University Press.

Heibronn, R. (2008) *Teacher Education and the Development of Practical Judgement*. London: Continuum.

Hill, W.F. (2002) *Learning: a Survey of Psychological Interpretation*. Boston: Allyn and Bacon.

King, S. (2000) *Into the Black Box: Observing Classrooms*. Sheffield: The Geographical Association.

Kyriacou, C. (1997) *Effective Teaching in Schools: Theory and Practice*. London: Nelson Thornes.

Lambert, D. and Balderstone, D. (2000) *Learning to Teach Geography in the Secondary School*. London: RoutledgeFalmer, pp. 414–419.

Lambert, D. and Sankey, D. (1994) 'Classrooms as ecosystems', *Journal of Teacher Development* 3(3): 175–181.

Leat, D. (1997) 'Cognitive acceleration in geographical education', in Tilbury, D. and Williams, M. (eds) *Teaching and Learning Geography*. London: Routledge, pp. 143–153.

Leat, D. (1998) *Thinking Through Geography*. Cambridge: Chris Kington Publishing.

Mezirow, J. (1990) *Fostering Critical Reflection in Adulthood: a Guide to Transformative and Emancipatory Learning*. San Francisco: Jossey-Bass.

Moon, J. (2004) *A Handbook of Reflective and Experiential Learning*. London: RoutledgeFalmer.

Moore, A. (2000) *Teaching and Learning: Pedagogy, Curriculum and Culture.* London and New York: RoutledgeFalmer.

Moore, A. (2004) *The Good Teacher.* London and New York: RoutledgeFalmer.

Nichols, A. and Leat, D. (2001) *More Thinking Through Geography.* Cambridge: Chris Kington Publishing.

Ofsted/TTA (Office for Standards in Education/Teacher Training Agency) (1996) *Framework for the Assessment of Quality and Standards in Initial Teacher Training 1996/7.* London: Ofsted.

Pask, R. and Joy, B. (2007) *Mentoring – Coaching: a Handbook for Education Professionals.* Oxford: Oxford University Press.

Robertson, J. (2005) *Coaching Leadership.* New Zealand: CER Press.

Roth, R. (1989) 'Preparing the reflective practitioner: transforming the apprentice through the dialectic', *Journal of Teacher Education* 40(2): 31–35.

Schön, D.A. (1987) *Educating the Reflective Practitioner.* San Francisco: Jossey Bass.

Schön, D.A. (1991) *The Reflective Practitioner: How Professionals Think in Action.* London: Temple Smith.

TDA (2007) 'Professional Standards for Teachers'. Online, available at: www.tda.gov.uk/teachers/professionalstandards/downloads.aspx (accessed 10 January 2009).

TDA (2008) Training and Development Agency for schools website. Online, available at: www.tda.gov.uk/teachers/mtl.aspx (accessed 22 June 2009).

Toh, Y.L.E. (2004) *Understanding Reflective Practice in Geography: Teachers' Views, its Role and Feasibility.* Unpublished MA Dissertation, Institute of Education, University of London.

Wragg, E.C. (1994) *An Introduction to Classroom Observation.* London: Routledge.

Zeichner, K.M. (1994) 'Research on teacher thinking and different views of reflective practice in teacher and teacher education', in Carlgren, I., Handal, G. and Vaage, S. (eds) *Teachers' Minds and Actions: Research of Teachers' Thinking and Practice.* London: The Falmer Press.

Part II

Dimensions of teaching geography

4   Making sense of the global dimension

The role of research

Nicole Blum, Douglas Bourn and Karen Edge

> We live in a global society and I believe it is important that young people, wherever they are in the world, have an understanding of how their actions and choices impact on the lives of others – not only in different countries but also on different continents. From the food we buy to the way we get to work, our everyday decisions have consequences for the world around us and we need to understand those consequences if we are to build a fairer, more sustainable society.
>
> (Gordon Brown, UK Prime Minister, in DEA 2008)

Learning and understanding about the wider world has always been part of the school curriculum, particularly within geography. But what is this learning about and why is it important? Any aspect of human geography that looks at diverse countries and places around the world today needs to locate learning within the context of a 'global sense of place'. In a globalised society, understanding about the wider world has to make reference to the interconnections of people and places, whether they live in London or Mumbai. This approach to geography builds on the field of learning called 'development education' or 'global education'. This field has predominantly been led by non-governmental organisations (NGOs) such as Oxfam, Christian Aid, UNICEF, ActionAid and Save the Children. Whilst the resources and the projects these organisations have created to support teachers have been well received, a focus on delivery of projects has meant that there has been little research to assess the value and contribution of development education to geographical learning.

The inclusion of the 'global dimension' to geography brings within it not just a recognition of globalisation and living in an interdependent world, but also – because it addresses issues such as global poverty, social inequalities and social justice – suggests that a key component of teaching about these areas in the classroom requires an understanding and recognition of a diverse range of social, cultural and ideological influences. Andreotti (2006), for example, suggests that from a post-colonial perspective the global dimension needs to include reference to how assumptions of cultural supremacy and North–South power relations are addressed. For example, discussions of poverty in the classroom can often instil perceptions of helplessness and charitable benevolence, rather than encouraging critical analysis of the reasons for global poverty and inequality.

On the other hand, as Standish (2009) suggests, the global dimension can also be perceived as promoting support for the particular ethical and moral positions of organisations such as Oxfam. So how can learning about global issues and forces include not just endorsing moral standpoints such as 'make poverty history' or 'being a global citizen', but also encourage critical thinking, understanding of different viewpoints and perspectives, and enable the learner to make sense of their relationship to global forces?

This chapter outlines the importance of research to teaching and learning about global and development issues, and discusses different theories, approaches and skills that are valuable in understanding processes of learning about the global dimension. It then relates these debates to the practice of development education and its contribution to geographical education. The chapter also argues that key to understanding the impact of the global dimension in the classroom is recognising and analysing the contribution of NGO-led resources and projects. It concludes by looking specifically at the global dimension in secondary geography, and suggesting ways that teacher-led classroom research can help teachers to develop a greater understanding of pupils' learning about the wider world.

The aims of this chapter are:

1   to demonstrate the need for classroom-based research that shows the contribution of the global dimension to geography.
2   to explore approaches to teacher-led research and identify which are the most appropriate to developing understandings of the impacts of learning about global and development issues within the classroom.
3   to outline the contribution that development education has already made to school geography as well as its potential contribution – e.g. enabling pupils to make sense of their relationship to global society – in the future.
4   to give examples of research approaches that can help to analyse how the global dimension is delivered in secondary geography, and to explore how children learn to make sense of their connections to global issues and concerns.

The contribution of development education to geography

The term 'development education' first emerged in the UK during the 1970s in part due to the influence of UNESCO, who promoted the term in relation to 'understanding of causes of underdevelopment and the promotion of what is involved in development' and made linkages to issues such as human rights and social justice (Osler 1994). The drivers for this agenda were NGOs and governments who were seeking public support and involvement in international aid and development.

During the 1980s, two broader influences began to have an impact on this emerging field of learning. The first was the thinking of the Brazilian educator, Paulo Freire, whose work emphasised participatory learning and the links between knowledge and social change. The second was the emergence of what Harrison (2005) calls the 'globalist' approach in the UK. This included the work of the World Studies Project, led by Robin Richardson and later Dave Hicks, Graham Pike and David Selby. The emphasis in their writings was on learning about the world, rather than a specific emphasis on poverty and development (Richardson 1976; Pike and Selby 1988; Hicks 1990, 2003).

These trends were mirrored in other industrialised countries, with NGOs increasingly playing the dominant role as government engagement rose and fell depending on political interest in aid and development. Throughout the 1980s and 1990s, the practice of development education in a range of industrialised countries focused on participatory learning about global and development issues and how this would lead to informed social action. Within the UK specifically, the driver for much of this practice was a growing network of local Development Education Centres who produced teaching and learning resources and also introduced models of learning through projects in partnerships with teachers and other educators.

Today these Centres promote an approach to learning about global and development issues that has moved a long way from the outline suggested by UNESCO in the 1970s. Teachers for Development Education (TIDE), an NGO based in Birmingham, for example, refers to sharing values about the potential role of education in building a positive future and through a process of learning responding to global issues.[1] Global Education Derby states that they work with teachers, youth workers and other educators

> to promote increased awareness of the importance of global citizenship in the lives of young people, and to offer opportunities for reflective, creative and innovative work that develops the themes of sustainable development within the policies and practices of the education system.[2]

MUNDI, a Centre based in Nottingham, states that its mission is to promote through 'education, a critical awareness, understanding and knowledge of global development, citizenship and sustainability issues in order to enact change towards a more equitable sustainable world'.[3] Behind these aims is recognition of the importance of critical thinking and a learner-centred approach to development education.

In relation to geographical education specifically, some of these Centres and NGOs such as Oxfam and ActionAid have produced resources that have become well-respected and popular among many teachers. Well-known examples include ActionAid's series of packs on Chembakolli, Oxfam's materials related to their framework of Education for Global Citizenship, various packs from TIDE using the 'Development Compass Rose' framework, and the 'Send My Friend to School' initiative co-ordinated by the

Global Campaign for Education. Themes such as fair trade and climate change, and the use of interactive approaches including role-plays, games and visual aids, are popular approaches in the resources produced for teachers.

The contribution of development education to geography therefore can be not only seen at the level of supportive resources, but also as a particular approach that emphasises the importance of learning about the linkages between development, globalisation and inequalities in the world today. Tony Binns (2000) argues that development education is an important component of geography because pupils need to understand about the causes of global inequalities and, especially in the UK, to be able to make sense of Britain's economic, social and cultural role in the world both today and in the past.

Another of development education's contributions to formal education is its attention to globalisation, global citizenship and the global dimension. Promoting educational strategies that take account of global society and the global economy are increasingly prevalent in the UK (DfES 2004) and other industrialised countries (Hertmeyer 2008; Rasaren 2009). There is also increasing rhetoric about promoting young people as global citizens, both within curriculum policy documents (e.g. QCA 2007) and in materials from NGOs (e.g. Oxfam 2006). However, whatever the influences and intentions of these statements and policies in terms of equipping learners to make sense of the wider world, the implementation can all too often be reduced to a descriptive analysis of globalisation and the (usually negative) consequences of living in an interconnected world. The QCA *Global Dimension in Action* publication is therefore significant because it states:

> Education for the global dimension encourages learners to evaluate information and events from a range of perspectives, to think critically about challenges facing the global community such as migration, identity and diversity, equality of opportunity and sustainability, and to explore some of the solutions to these issues.
>
> (QCA 2007: 2)

This expansion of support for the global dimension within the school curriculum has not been mirrored by research and evidence to demonstrate its contribution to broader educational agendas in terms of raising standards, contribution to community cohesion or equipping young people to be active participants in society.

Towards a theory of learning

As already mentioned in this chapter, much of the drive for the inclusion of global and development issues within the curriculum, including geography, has come from NGOs. This has resulted in an emphasis on delivering projects, producing resources and in some cases securing support for specific campaigns and issues such as fair trade, climate change or poverty. This normative approach has been criticised by Scheunpflug and Asbrand (2006) and posed alongside the need for a critical approach by Vare and Scott (2008) in relation to sustainable development. An example of this can be seen through the Fair Trade Foundation's promotion of an awards programme for schools. Although it can be beneficial, schools' efforts to win the award can also result in an uncritical endorsement of fair trade by teachers and, as a consequence, pupils may be left without opportunities for critical discussion and debate. Promoting fair trade as a unquestionably good thing or as the only solution to the problems of world trade is far too simplistic.

The need for a more critically engaged approach to learning about global and development issues has emerged through the initiative Open Space for Dialogue and Enquiry (OSDE) and the parallel programme Through Other Eyes (TOE). Both programmes were the result of activities developed by Development Education Centres in the East Midlands of England in partnership with Nottingham University.

The OSDE methodology supports the creation of open and safe spaces for dialogue and enquiry about global issues where 'people are invited to engage critically with their own and with different perspectives, think independently and make informed and responsible decisions about how they want to think and what they want to do'.[4]

The Through Other Eyes initiative similarly aims to support educators to develop a 'set of tools to reflect on their own knowledge systems and to engage with other knowledge systems in different ways, in their own learning and in their classrooms'. As two of the programme's creators comment:

> TOE was designed to enable educators to develop an understanding of how language and systems of belief, values and representation affect the way people interpret the world, to identify how different groups understand issues related to development and their implications for the development agenda and to critically examine these interpretations both 'Western' and 'indigenous'.
>
> (Andreotti and de Souza 2008: 23–24)

These initiatives were critiqued by students at the Institute on Education undertaking the Masters course in Development Education. In their feedback, many of the students commented that it represented an important contribution to work in the area, and also that it proved to be a productive learning experience for them individually. As one student noted:

> Educational interventions such as TOE, which seek to challenge our current systems of thought, are essential if we are to move beyond superficial forms of global citizenship which leave the origins of our perceptions, values and assumptions unquestioned and potentially reinforce mainstream ideas.
>
> (Extract from assignment 2008)

Global dimension in geography in the classroom

An example of an approach to addressing learning about global and development issues within the secondary geography curriculum specifically is the publication *Geography: the Global Dimension*, produced by the Geographical Association in partnership with the DEA. This publication poses an approach that moves beyond 'development indicators' and 'case studies' by encouraging 'geographical imaginations' and 'understanding of the interconnections between places and scales' (Lambert *et al.* 2004).

Standish (2009) has criticised this publication because it is promoting an approach to geography that devalues the traditional subject-based knowledge and promotes a value-laden perspective with specific agendas. However, his critique fails to address the interests and needs of the learner: to understand and make sense of global issues and concerns, individuals must develop skills to enable them to make connections between their own lives and people elsewhere in the world, and to critically assess their own prejudices and perspectives in the light of the views of others. Key to the global dimension in geography teaching in the classroom is moving beyond notions of learning *about* development in a detached and normative form, to one that poses and encourages debates about complex questions and issues that have no easy solutions. It also means encouraging a process of learning that recognises existing prejudices and perspectives, that moves from learning to unlearn, to learning to listen, to learning to learn and learning to reach out (Andreotti and de Souza 2008).

The resource pack *How Do We Know it's Working? A Toolkit for Measuring Attitudinal Change in Global Citizenship* (RISC 2008), produced by a Development Education Centre based in Reading, Berkshire, provides a useful example of a process that encourages teachers and students to move from a charity perspective of development to one of interdependence and recognition of external economic, social and ideological influences.

One activity in the pack, for instance, looks at how perceptions of Africa may have changed as a result of critical learning – of moving beyond stereotypes to an understanding of the causes of the poverty. A number of UK schools have already used this toolkit, and the results give a mixed picture, often related to both schools' level of commitment and the influence of external factors. In two of the six schools in which it has been used, the principles the activity was seeking to embed, including notions of social justice, equity and action for change, were not realised. In some cases this was because the topic was seen as a 'bolt-on and extra to ongoing curricula activity' (Lowe 2008: 64). When this was the case, there was no measurable change in pupils' attitudes, and responses to some activities indicated that pupils' stereotypical attitudes had actually been reinforced.

Another activity in the pack is designed to find out 'what pupils think and know about action they can take to make the world a more just and sustainable place' (RISC 2008: 23). In a mainly white, rural primary school, the activity was conducted by asking the 'pupils to write, talk or draw pictures of anything that they could think of that could be their individual action' (RISC 2008: 27) Their responses were divided up into four categories: local sustainability, global sustainability, local social justice and global social justice (RISC 2008: 28). The main outcomes of this activity were a common failure to distinguish between local and global, and a weakness in thinking about the lives of people around the world, with a charitable perception being the dominant one. Following an in-depth programme of support to teachers based around themes such as causes of poverty, fair trade and human rights, a more balanced outcome emerged with more emphasis on the importance of access to resources, resolving conflict and concepts of fairness and social justice (RISC 2008: 29).

The role of research

These examples of practice re-enforce the important of research for teaching and learning about global and development issues. There is a great deal of practice in this area, led predominately by NGOs. There is increased policy support for the global dimension and there is an emerging discourse around theories of learning on global and development education. But what have not, as yet, emerged, are a number of empirically based studies on what and how teaching and learning about global and development issues looks like within the classroom.

Research is therefore a key need for building support and understanding about teaching of global and development issues. First, it provides the researcher (in this case, the teacher) and the research participants (this could be students, parents, fellow teachers or others) with a critical space for reflec-tion on particular ideas, concepts and practices. Second, when research is shared (either formally or informally) it helps to build a body of knowledge about those ideas and practices, which can inform future thinking and approaches. This is especially the case in the field of global and development education, which is a relatively small – although growing – area of work.

In order to encourage this critical space as part of the research process, however, attention has to be paid to the kinds of methods and approaches used. While surveys and questionnaires can be useful for gathering large amounts of 'data', for instance, they provide little in the way of context for understanding why people give particular answers to set questions. To provide a simple example: if someone answers 'yes' to the question 'do you think it is a good idea to recycle?', there may be no way of knowing if this is the respondent's real opinion or if they simply think that it is the 'right' answer according to social rules and norms. This is not to say that surveys are not useful research methods, but rather that they can be much more illuminating when used in combination with other methods. If a researcher also spends time interacting with research participants and uses reflexive and participatory research methods, for example, they are more likely to be able to develop an in-depth understanding of the issues and practices they are investigating.

Teachers are in a particularly strong position to conduct this kind of research in classrooms because they will already be familiar with classroom, school and community contexts, and may have known the research participants (their own students, parents, fellow teachers, school managers, etc.) for some time. Teachers also stand to benefit significantly from an engagement with research because it can provide important opportunities for critical reflection on specific concepts/ ideas/curricula, on student learning and on their own practice.

Researching practice

Relevant research into the practice and impact of the global dimension can take place within individual classrooms, across an entire school or networks of schools. Research can also be designed to capture an instance in the learning process, track development of learning and attitudinal change over time. Research into the global dimension can also be led by teachers and students. We believe strongly that the best research is relevant to the task at hand and creates opportunities for reflection on the findings that can be channelled into future learning.

However, research can fall short of the wider goal of enriching the education community's understanding of the influence of the global dimension on attitudes, knowledge and skills. Many times, this is because there has been little time or resource to 'dig deep' into the issues and knowledge that precede learning or result from a particular instructional unit. However, as we show below, examples from the classroom level, the whole school or network of schools level can demonstrate how to harness the information on learning and perceptions related to the global dimension.

Within classrooms

Often, gathering data on how individuals perceived and/or have experienced particular issues at the beginning of a unit of instruction can be very helpful. However, using this data against data collected at the end of the unit can be used as an instructional tool itself to identify future areas of study, how the individuals have moved their thinking forward (or not!) and how to critically analyse and reflect on their participation in the unit.

For example, students can be engaged in creating mind maps of their current knowledge, attitudes and perceptions of a particular issue like global warming. For the second stage of data gathering, they can identify where they learnt each piece of information and if it has influenced their behaviour or thinking. At the end of the unit, students can engage in creating a new 'map' and then comparing it to the one they first drew. Using both maps to reflect on their learning and how they will take their learning forward is a helpful way to create an evidence base of what learning occurred and students' reflection upon it. Scaling this individual activity to the classroom level, the whole class can be engaged in creating a larger map that highlights each of the issues that were identified and indicating the number of people in the class who had noted them down. Students themselves can be engaged in creating strategies for monitoring what they have learnt and how it has changed their thinking as a class.

Across classrooms or schools

One of the best ways to develop practice and expertise is to work across class-rooms and schools to share knowledge and experience between teachers and students. One strategy commonly used in knowledge-management and learn-ing communities is called a 'knowledge exchange' or a 'learning fair'. This involves a group of individuals all preparing a similar report on their work and coming together to share their experience. It can involve table displays and short presentations on each piece of work. Events like this require some preparation by the teacher and students, but they have been found to be incredibly helpful at sharing knowledge and building relationships.

It is also common at these events to have participants prepare a written summary of their work. Prior to or after the event, these summaries can be collated to create an overall evidence base and resource that shares the col-lective wisdom and learning of the group.

Concluding comments

This chapter has outlined the contribution development education can play to geography education. As the global dimension has an increasingly important contribution within all aspects of teaching and education, there is a need for this space to be more than just learning about far-away places. In the era of globalisation and an interdependent world, but one that is still influenced by inequalities, learning about issues such as poverty must include references to social, economic and ideological influences on perceptions about people and places.

This therefore provides an important opportunity for teacher-led research that includes studying ways in which pupils learn about global and develop-ment issues, what influences their learning and what role the teacher can play in challenging preconceived notions and stereotypes. The development edu-cation approach can, if it includes a critical-learning perspective and moves beyond just reproducing NGO-led resource activities in the classroom, play an important contribution to a new approach to geographical education.

Dissertation summary

Alison Leonard (2004) 'School Linking and Geography'

One of the most popular ways in which schools are encouraged to support pupils' understanding of global and development issues is through a link with a school elsewhere in the world. Alison Leonard's dissertation aims to address the value of linking in the context of its benefits to enquiry learning, how links are brought into the classroom and if the process of linking alters the nature and learning about development. For Leonard a motivation was to address the extent to which linking reinforced negative stereotypes about developing countries.

In reviewing the literature on school linking, Leonard noted that much of it was related to reporting on current practice through the activities of supporting organisations such as the British Council, United Kingdom One World Linking Association (UKOWLA) and local Development Education Centres. She notes particularly the recognition by some commentators on linking and partnerships of the dangers of a one-way flow of experience from the North to the South. Key to her observations on current school-linking practice is the questioning that it is about 'equality and reciprocity' because of the unequal relationships that exist between Northern and Southern schools. This does not mean that the partnership cannot be valuable, it is just that the aims and needs are likely to be different.

Leonard noted four main reasons why UK schools form links:

- To develop new teaching resources.
- To foster improved understanding of ethnicity and multi-culturalism.
- To promote global citizenship.
- In response to a desire to help partners materially.

In reviewing existing literature and knowledge on these reasons, Leonard identified a range of materials that demonstrated the value of linking towards these aims, but also found evidence of Northern dominance in decision-making and unintended paternalism.

To address her research questions with geography teachers, Leonard used a combination of quantitative and qualitative data collection. To gather evidence of the extent to which schools were using linking in a comparative form, she used a survey to known schools engaged in links and, through PGCE geography students, those schools that did not have links.

Questionnaires were also used with the pupils from the three schools. These questionnaires were conducted with Year 9 pupils from three schools to see what differences emerged between those who had experienced some form of link and those that had not.

To gain a more detailed insight into the linking process, Leonard chose a qualitative technique of semi-structured interviews with teachers from the schools that have links. The differences could then be explored further through semi-structured interviews with teachers from the schools.

The findings from her research were as follows:

- There are statistically significant differences in views on several aspects of development between pupils from linked and non-linked schools from within her sample. But she notes that because she used a questionnaire from an NGO – VSO – which has its own 'agenda', there was evidence of a built-in bias within the survey.

- Geography teachers' perceptions of pupils learning about development issues *were* also significantly different between linked and non-linked schools. However she notes that her results came from a small, self-selecting sample and that the process of obtaining questionnaire responses proved to be problematic. Similar responses and observations were made in response to teaching global citizenship within schools.

- The case studies within the schools were the most successful part of the research process. Those interviewed considered linking an important element of their school community. In the rural schools with mainly white pupils, linking provided an opening to discussions on cultural and ethnic diversity.

Finally, in reviewing her findings, Leonard undertook a SWOT analysis (strengths, weaknesses, opportunities and threats). The strengths included identification of positive and negative attributes of developing countries, developing empathy with people in these countries and improving communication skills, Above all, she noted that, if organised well, linking can encourage critical thinking, problem-solving and identify ways in which pupils can bring about change. However, on a negative side, linking can promote a re-enforcing of stereotypes, a dependency culture and lead to conflicting aims and misunderstandings. These observations relate also to comments made earlier in this chapter (Lowe 2008). In terms of opportunities, linking can bring development alive and enable areas such as race and culture to be raised within the geography classroom. It can also be an opportunity to bring ICT into the classroom. Threats included misuse of funding and resources, competing demands from other initiatives and political pressures, particularly on Southern partners.

Leonard's dissertation conclusions, which have subsequently been developed (Leonard 2008), suggest that whilst linking can be a valuable contribution to learning about development issues within geography, it does bring with it a number of wider social, cultural and ideological perspectives that need to be recognised. Also, since the dissertation was completed in 2004, there has been a considerable expansion of both resources and research on linking (Edge and Jaafar 2008; Martin 2008) that further demonstrate whilst linking can enrich a pupils' understanding of development issues, the influence of postcolonialism cannot be ignored (Andreotti 2006). Leonard's research identified the value of direct dialogue and contact with both teachers and pupils, but that the results and evidence need to be viewed in a comparative sense and situated within the broader discourses on development education and learning about global and development issues.

For discussion

- Within the context of recognising this is an under-researched area, what are the key areas that are a priority in terms of research on the global dimension and geography?

- To what extent is there still a need to look at the relationships between what children learn in the classroom about topics such as global poverty and climate change and the influence of the media, peer groups and the community in terms of perceptions about these areas? This is an area explored in Leonard's dissertation in relation to the perceptions many pupils may have about developing countries.
- As this chapter has identified, NGOs have played a key role in influencing the global dimension within the classroom. As teachers grow in confidence and experience on the global dimension, is there a need to look at processes in the development of teachers' own confidence, skills and knowledge?

Further reading

1 Bourn, D. (ed.) (2008) *Development Education: Debates and Dialogues*. London: Bedford Way Papers. This is a useful text to introduce the issues and debates around Development Education.
2 Burton, D. and Bartlett, S. (2005) *Practitioner Research for Teachers*. London: Paul Chapman. For teachers who wish to research their practice, this text gives some useful advice on how to proceed.
3 Lambert, D., Morgan, A., Swift, D. and Brownlie, A. (2004) *Geography: the Global Dimension*. London: DEA/Geographical Association. This publication explores the relationship between the global dimension and the subject of geography, and is a must for every geography teacher.

Notes

1 www.tidec.org/Aims/Tide%7e-aims.html.
2 www.globaleducationderby.org.uk.
3 www.mundi.org.uk/what-is-mundi/index.html.
4 www.osdemethodology.org.uk/osdemethodology.html.

References

Andreotti, V. (2006) A Postcolonial Reading of Contemporary Discourses Related to the Global Dimension in Education in England. PhD Thesis, University of Nottingham.

Andreotti, V. and de Souza, L.M. (2008) 'Translating theory into practice and walking minefields: lessons from the project "Through Other Eyes"', *International Journal of Development Education and Global Learning*, 1(1): 23–36.

Binns, T. (2000) 'Learning about development: an entitlement for all', in Binns, T. and Fisher, C. (eds) *Issues in Geography Teaching*. London: RoutledgeFalmer.

Burton, D. and Bartlett, S. (2005) *Practitioner Research for Teachers*. London: Paul Chapman.

DEA (Development Education Association) (2008) *Global Matters Learning – Case Studies*. London: DEA.

DfES (2004) *Putting the World into World Class Education*. London: DfES.

Edge, K. and Jaafar, S.B. (2008) *North–South School Partnerships: Learning from Schools in the UK, Africa and Asia*. Research report, Year 1. London: London Centre for Leadership in Learning, Institute of Education, University of London.

Harrison, D. (2005) 'Post-Its on the history of development education', *Development Education Journal*, 13(1): 6–8.

Hertmeyer, H. (2008) *Experiencing the World – Global Learning in Austria: Developing, Reaching Out, Crossing Borders*. Münster: Waxmann.

Hicks, D. (1990) 'World studies 8–13: a short history, 1980–89', *Westminster Studies in Education*, 13: 61–80.

Hicks, D. (2003) 'Thirty years of global education', *Educational Review*, 55(3): 265–275.

Hicks, D. and Holden, C. (eds) (2007) *Teaching the Global Dimension*. London: Routledge.

Lambert, D., Morgan, A., Swift, D. and Brownlie, A. (2004) *Geography: the Global Dimension*. London: DEA/Geographical Association.

Leonard, A. (2008) 'Global School Relationships: school linking and modern challenges', in Bourn, D. (ed.) *Development Education Debates and Dialogues*. London: Bedford Way Papers.

Lowe, B. (2008) 'Embedding global citizenship in primary and secondary schools: developing a methodology for measuring attitudinal change', *International Journal of Development Education and Global Learning*, 1(1): 59–64.

Martin, F. (2008) 'Mutual learning: the impact of a study visit course on UK teachers' knowledge and understanding of global partnerships', *Critical Literacy: Theories and Practices*, 2(1): 60–75.

Osler, A. (ed.) (1994) *Development Education*. London: Cassells.

Oxfam (2006) *Education for Global Citizenship*. Oxford: Oxfam.

Pike, G. and Selby, D. (1988) *Global Teacher, Global Learner*. Sevenoaks: Hodder & Stoughton.

QCA (Qualifications and Curriculum Authority) (2007) *Global Dimension in Action*. London: QCA.

Rasaren, R. (2009) 'Transformative global education and learning in teacher education in Finland', *International Journal of Development Education and Global Learning*, 1(2).

Richardson, R. (1976) *Learning for Change in World Society*. London: World Studies Project.

RISC (2008) *How Do We Know it's Working? A Toolkit for Measuring Attitudinal Change in Global Citizenship*. Reading: RISC.

Scheunpflug, A. and Asbrand, B. (2006) 'Global education and education for sustainability', *Environmental Education Research*, 12(1): 33–46.

Standish, A. (2009) *Global Perspectives in the Geography Curriculum: Reviewing the Moral Case for Geography*. London: Routledge.

Vare, P. and Scott, W. (2008) Education for Sustainable Development: Two Sides and an Edge. DEA Thinkpiece. Online, available from: www.dea.org.uk/think-pieces.

5 Developing and reflecting on subject expertise

Clare Brooks

Trends in education place demands on teachers to navigate their way through a maze of advice, strategies and official guidance and expectations. In order to respond to this complex context, Morgan and Lambert (2005) advocate the 'scholarship of teaching'. This is an attractive but elusive term. This chapter explores what 'scholarly teaching' means in schools, and in particular how it relates to subject knowledge. Subject knowledge is often closely associated with teachers' identity in secondary schools, but paradoxically is not always at the heart of teachers' CPD (continuing professional development) or thinking. The focus of this chapter is to illustrate the importance of subject knowledge in scholarly teaching and demonstrate how engagement with subject expertise can influence practice.

The aims of this chapter are:

- to explore one interpretation of scholarly teaching.
- to understand what role subject expertise plays in the development of scholarly teaching.
- to consider how teachers can use their geographical expertise in their planning and teaching.

Subject contents

The importance of subject knowledge in relation to other dimensions of geography teachers' work is not a simple issue. In 1997 Marsden published a paper called 'On taking the geography out of geography education'. Marsden suggests there are three components to education: education (the Method), social education (the Mission) and the subject (the Matter). He argues that for education to be successful all three should be in balance. Over-emphasis on any one distorts the educative process. For example, too much emphasis on pedagogy (the Method) means that young people do lots of exciting things, but don't actually end up learning much; what Morgan and Lambert (2005) call the 'pedagogic adventure'. Marsden argues that the emphasis on issues in geography education in the 1980s placed too much focus on the Mission and the Method and consequently were light on the Matter – making the learning here less geographical (and more sociological).

Marsden's argument can be applied to trends in geography education since the publication of his paper. For example, the Original Orders of the National Curriculum was highly prescriptive, focusing on 'content' to be covered. The Programme of Study for the Original National Curriculum was a list of geographical content presented without curriculum aims or a subject-based rationale. Subsequently, teachers were unclear why this content was chosen, how the elements were linked and how they represented a curriculum-planning tool. Lambert (2004) argues that teachers consequently focused on covering the content listed in the GNC, rather than the geographical concepts that linked them. Note the emphasis here on content rather than the subject. Lambert records four effects that emerged as a consequence of this content-heavy curriculum:

- Control over what is taught was perceived to come from outside the specialist teaching community.
- It is presumed that school geography had to 'cover' in approximate balance the full range of what is geography – the human, the physical, the environmental, the regional.
- It was taken as given that geography is essentially 'content rich' – an empirical account of the earth's features, or mimesis.
- Despite lip-service paid to techniques to promote 'enquiry learning', geography fundamentally fulfilled the requirements of an 'answer culture' (2004: 78).

The Original Orders of the National Curriculum had an impact on both the content covered and how it was taught, demonstrating what can occur when the three components that Marsden identified are out of balance. The way that subject content was defined had a significant impact not on what was taught but how it was taught. Lambert's analysis shows that the national curriculum prevented some teachers from using their subject expertise to develop their local curriculum.

The Geography National Curriculum has changed substantially since the 1991 Orders (having been revised in 1995, 2000 and 2008) and yet this analysis is worthwhile. The 'hangover' from the Original Orders is still prevalent in some geography departments today (often preserved by investing heavily in a textbook series that structures curriculum coverage). We can learn a valuable lesson from this era. How a school subject is understood, and how the curriculum is described, can have an impact on how it is taught. Graves calls this the 'curriculum problem' which he defines as: 'what shall be taught in school, in what framework, with what methods and how evaluation of the learning may take place' (1979: 104).

To resolve these questions, teachers need to draw upon both their subject expertise and their detailed knowledge of their students.

Scholarly teaching

In their exploration of curriculum development, Morgan and Lambert (2005) note how curriculum planning requires that teachers have secure subject knowledge. One view of lesson planning is that it converts teachers' subject knowledge into a meaningful form for students. This transmission-style model assumes that the subject content is somehow fixed (and resides in the teacher's head). The lesson-planning process becomes about how the subject knowledge is presented rather than what is covered, placing the focus on teaching skills and pedagogy rather than on students' learning. Not only does this approach neglect the dynamic and problematic nature of geographical knowledge production, but also the role that students have to play in developing and constructing their own geographical knowledge (Morgan and Lambert 2005).

Morgan and Lambert look at four examples of curriculum planning, asking questions about what is being taught and the rationale for teaching it. It is in their summary of the QCA scheme of work that they refer to scholarly teaching:

> The QCA unit 'Crime and the Community' provides a stark example of why a scholarly approach to lesson planning is necessary. The unit provides a ready-made answer to the question of what and how to teach about crime. It can be used by geography teachers to construct lessons but does not require them to think about what lessons to construct. It does not offer a rationale for curriculum selection. Without an explicit understanding that geographical knowledge is a social construction, teachers are not in a position to assess and evaluate the geography they are asked to teach, and they are unlikely to find ways to alert students to other ways of making sense of the topic, other ways of viewing the world.
>
> (Morgan and Lambert 2005: 91)

Their argument links scholarly teaching with the process of curriculum planning and preparation. They note that a 'given' curriculum such as a published scheme of work can prevent a teacher from thinking through what they are teaching and why this is important or relevant for their students. So, what do they mean by a 'scholarly approach' and how can teachers achieve this?

The notion of the scholarship of teaching was introduced in the debate concerning Scholarship in Higher Education. In 1990, Boyer published an influential argument urging the academy to broaden understood notions of scholarship. His argument was that valuing academics for their research work alone neglected appreciation of the other valuable dimensions of their work (Boyer 1990). He identified four areas of scholarship: discovery, integration, application and teaching, which, when taken together, demonstrate that academics achieve more than just 'discovery' or research. Academics are also influential in how their 'discovery' is applied, disseminated and ultimately taken on by others. Research doesn't occur in a vacuum. Boyer argued that research is enhanced through its application, sharing it with others, and teaching it.

The development of the Scholarship of Teaching (or the Scholarship of Teaching and Learning as it is now known (Hutchings and Shulman 1999)) is also of particular interest to teachers not located in the higher-education sector. Boyer's (1990) analysis notes that teaching is more than transmitting knowledge, but also the process of teaching transforms and extends it. Therefore this understanding of teaching (although in Higher Education) goes beyond the interactions that take place in the classroom and into an understanding of teaching that is grounded in intellectual endeavour and considered decision-making. Hutchings and Shulman describe this as 'a broader, more capacious meaning', that 'requires a kind of "going meta"' (1999: 13).

This broad definition of scholarly teaching is valuable for teachers in a school context as it is grounded in notions of teachers' professionalism (see Chapter 1). Morgan and Lambert argued that using 'off-the-shelf' curriculum development uncritically, as exemplified by the QCA scheme of work, projects implicit notions of what it means to be a teacher. Accepting that QCA published these schemes as part of their remit to support teachers, the danger is that some teachers may have understood this as being the model curriculum and implemented them uncritically (as evidenced in the 2008 Ofsted report). In this instance, teachers are acting as technicians, 'delivering' the curriculum, and delegating decisions to the scheme of work author about what to teach and how. Smith and Girod (2003) have noted that this is often a consequence when teachers use pre-prepared teaching units. They argue it is a reductionist view of teaching, which severely limits the capacity of the teacher to act as a professional, not least because the curriculum publisher does not have knowledge of the teacher's particular students.

It is this dimension of teaching individual students that makes teaching so rewarding and challenging. Further investigation into the Scholarship of Teaching focusing on this relationship can help us to explain this process further. In particular, synoptic capacity focuses on the relationship between subject knowledge and students. Understanding synoptic capacity places emphasis on teachers using their subject expertise to connect with their students. Rice originally used the term in his analysis of the Scholarship of Teaching (1992). His definition is important because it shows how teachers' use of their subject knowledge should be located within:

1   their understanding of the subject as a whole;
2   their understanding of their students and their needs.

The definition reads:

> the ability to draw strands of a field together in a way that provides both coherence and meaning, to place what is known in context and opens the way for connections to be made between the knower and the known.
>
> (Rice 1992: 125)

This definition of synoptic capacity places emphasis on the teacher using their subject knowledge to connect what they are teaching with their students and their unique needs.

To exemplify what this means in practice, it is useful to refer to some examples of teaching where the 'coherence and meaning' that enables the knower and the known to connect are absent. In a recent paper (Brooks 2006), I critically examine three geography lessons, focusing on how the teacher has presented the geography of the lesson to the students. One lesson on acid rain emphasised the 'science' behind how acid rain is formed. The spatial component of the issue, i.e., how pollution in one location can affect places somewhere else, was not emphasised. This spatial connection is a difficult one to make without specialist geographical support. Without this spatial dimension, the issue is more science than geography.

However, when teachers do emphasise their subject expertise, they can make valuable connections between the subject content and their students. In my research, I have observed 'expert' geography teachers use three strategies to do this. The three strategies are:

- making connections with other geographical knowledge or experiences;
- tuning into the students' personal geographies;
- using the teacher's own geographical experiences to help students make links with similar or related phenomena.

These three strategies are predominantly focused on classroom interactions between teacher and student.

Subject expertise in lesson planning

To explore this further, it is useful to explore the thinking processes that teachers undergo to plan lessons. The next section includes extracts from a PGCE Masters level assignment that shows how the teacher, Emily, has justified what she is teaching within the context of its geographical value and also what it means for her students (the knower and the known).

Emily was teaching a scheme of work on Japan. Here she thinks through what her students already know about Japan and what sort of geographical knowledge she thinks they need to develop:

> As the unit was a case study of just one country, it was essential that the pupils developed their understanding about Japan as a *place*, dispelling their previous conceptions about what the country was like. Prior to this unit, each pupil had their own experiences with Japan, the majority of which had been shaped through mainstream television and film. It was therefore my intention that this scheme of work broaden the pupil's geographical imaginations, taking them beyond the constraints of their vicarious experiences. However, *place* is a complex concept, particularly when

boundaries and scale need to be taken into considering; how far does the identity of a place extend? One of the difficulties that I found was how to liberate the pupils' perception of Japan as a place without making generalisations myself. This is something that Wellsted (2006) highlights as one of the 'challenges' for geography teachers and suggests that we should '… use the study of place meaningfully … to help [our students] to acquire skills of critical thinking so that they can look beyond stereotypes …' (Wellsted 2006: 161). A way that I found to incorporate this was to encourage the pupils to engage with the topics covered through an enquiry based approach, creating the opportunity for them to begin to form their own connections with the topic.

Emily continues to consider how she can introduce her students to the idea that what they think they know about Japan may not be true:

> The cultural and social aspects taught in lessons 1 and 2 worked well as an introduction to Japan, and provided examples of how life here can be very different to our own experiences; but I was also concerned that to a certain extent they reaffirmed the stereotypes that as geography teachers we try to avoid. However, Dove (1999) has suggested that this method of building on the already existing perceptions of pupils can work well in introducing new ideas in geography. I developed Lesson 3 in accordance with this by showing an episode of *The Simpsons* which focuses on a family trip to Japan. Here I provided pupils with the opportunity to watch the programme critically, highlighting the stereotypes that were portrayed about Japan as a place, and how generalisations can be cast about places when our experience of them is limited, using stereotypes of England as a further example. This idea is supported by Dove (1999) who says that 'By anticipating potential "alternative conceptions" [or *preconceptions*], teachers can plan learning opportunities to develop students' understanding while avoiding, rather than compounding, misunderstandings' (Dove 1999: 35).

Having considered how she can explore generalisations about Japan, Emily then considers that the next building block is to get the students to understand the influence of the physical geography of Japan:

> In teaching about *place* there is also the need to explore the physical geography of the area that is being studied so that the influence and relevance of its location can be understood. This requires awareness on a broader scale, exploring what Massey (1995) suggests are the *relational* concepts of local, regional and global boundaries. Exploring these scales in reference to Japan as a *place* at an early stage provided me with the opportunity to lay the foundations for later lesson episodes which would develop on the relevance of location. This is something that Brooks and Morgan (2006) suggest is significant because '…different scales reveal different geographical

forces at work' (Brooks and Morgan 2006: 18). Lesson 3 acted as an introduction to the regions of Japan on a national scale, and demonstrated how
these are physically defined.... this was further developed in Lesson 4
where Japan's location was explored in a more complex global context,
which was again to be used a reference point in subsequent lessons.... The
significance of studying the country on this larger scale also means that
there is the opportunity to be aware of the interaction between Japan and
other nations. However to achieve a 'deep' understanding of place Brooks
and Morgan (2006) argue that as well as an appreciation of scale and
boundaries, the significance of historical events upon these also needs to be
considered (Brooks and Morgan 2006: 20).

Further analysis of Emily's rationale may lead us to question whether any
understanding of a distant place can be developed without it being based on
generalisations, or indeed to what extent relating the physical geography of an
area can be extrapolated into notions of environmental determinism.
However, what is important in the above extracts is that Emily is not shying
away from these complex issues. She has reflected on them within her own
context, and their applicability to the students she is teaching. She has also
sought advice from readings (both from the fields of geography education and
geography), and she has endeavoured to bring this understanding together in
her planning. It is her consideration of her students and their needs with her
geographical expertise that makes this planning scholarly.

Balancing the knower and the known

Central to the planning process is the consideration of the students, and what
is relevant and appropriate for them. This issue is tackled in detail in *Living
Geography* (Mitchell 2009). This edited collection presents an argument that
geography teachers need to connect with students' lived experiences and their
personal geographies. This emphasis on the student and their experiences is a
key feature of the work of John Dewey (1972) who argued that teachers
should use the experiences of pupils as the starting point for the curriculum.
Dewey's argument is worth considering in more detail.

Dewey argued that young people's learning starts with their experience. As
they encounter new phenomena, their understanding grows as they refer back
to their experience. Dewey describes this as 'psychological'. He contrasts this
process of how people learn to the way that subject disciplines are organised.
Subjects, he argues, are the products of many generations of thought and discovery. In order to organise all this previous work, subjects are structured in a logical
way. For a subject expert, this logical organisation is useful because ideas can be
penetrated quickly and easily. It also enables new knowledge to be mapped onto
the pre-existing bodies of knowledge. This is how teachers understand geography when they enter teaching. However, Dewey argues that it is not appropriate to structure a curriculum in this way, because it is not how students learn.

Dewey warns that a school curriculum that is structured in this way is in danger of being purely formal and symbolic. It may not connect with students' experience and so will require modification. Despite these arguments, Scott (2008) notes that most government- or state-based curriculum is expressed in this logical, subject-based way – often expressed, he argues, through narrowly defined behavioural objectives. Therefore, defining any subject through a series of learning objectives organised in a logical way (i.e. driven by the subject) will not help children to learn.

This is not to argue that the subject should not play an important role in deciding what is to be taught. Dewey, sometimes acknowledged as a key influence on the child-centred movement, has been wrongly criticised for neglecting the importance of subjects (Pring 2007). Pring notes that Dewey was not arguing that subjects are unimportant, but that they should not be the starting point for organising a curriculum. The implication of this for geography teachers is significant, as it requires an engagement with their subject from a different perspective. Teachers, as subject experts, need to reconsider and re-view their subject knowledge through the lens of their students and their experience. The curriculum developments and constraints in England and Wales in recent years have made this difficult to accomplish. As Emily has demonstrated above, this requires a deliberate consideration of how to move students from where they are (their current experience) to where the teacher wants them to be (the geography to be learnt).

In the dissertation summary that follows this chapter, Denise Freeman takes on the idea that the subject geography is constructed, and explores to what extent this construction is informed by the students that it is intended to connect with. As you read the dissertation summary you might like to consider:

1   To what extent can you exhibit scholarly teaching when using a geography textbook?
2   How is your geography curriculum informed by the needs and experiences of your students?
3   How can you increase your synoptic capacity, and explore new ways to enable students to connect their experiences with the geography you are teaching them?

Dissertation summary

Denise Freeman (2006) 'Constructing Geographical Worlds: an Investigation into the Construction of School Geography'

Freeman's dissertation has been chosen to accompany this chapter as it critically questions what is taught through school geography and why. The research was inspired by several popular geography texts such as *Fast Food Nation* (Schlosser 2002), *No Logo* (Klein 2001) and *The Corporation* (Achbar and Abbott, dir. 2004), which encouraged Freeman to consider how controversial geographical

topics were being handled in schools, how they were being presented and sim-
plified so that students could understand them, and subsequently how such
topics were constituting geographical knowledge in classrooms.

In her literature review, Freeman considers the historical development of
geography, how it has been constructed and the dominant ideologies that
have influenced this process. She identifies how this development in the academic subject has affected school geography, and the contrasting ideologies
that underpin those representations. Then, turning her attention to geography
textbooks as a key source of geographical information, Freeman identifies
three 'worlds' that feature in the study of school geography:

- the 'World' in which we live;
- the 'Geographical World' that is represented in school geography;
- the local, personal 'worlds' of the young people studying geography.

She questions how each of the geographical worlds that makes up school
geography is constructed and to what extent it is influenced by the 'youth
worlds'.

For her methodology, Denise adopts an interpretative approach. Borrowing
from phenomenology, she wants to understand how these worlds were constructed. Therefore, she identifies four influential 'actors' in the construction of
school geography, including a geography-education academic, a textbook
author, an A-level chief examiner and a policy-maker. Her chosen method of
data collection is to interview each of these actors about their involvement in
the construction of school geography. A key consideration in her methodology
is the ethics of such an approach. Often participants in research remain anony-
mous to protect their identity. However, in this research that would neither be
possible nor desirable, therefore due consideration is made to ensure the participants understand the costs of their participation.

In analysing her results, Freeman adopts a coding strategy. This enables her to
search for meanings both in the interview responses but also across the four
interviews as well. She therefore presents her results under four headings as to
what the participants told her about: Geography, School Geography, Constructing Geographical Knowledge, and Youth Worlds and School Geography. This
approach enables her to record key influences for each individual as well as
similarities and differences across the group. In her discussion, Freeman also
presents some of the responses in tabular form so they can be compared and
contrasted.

In her conclusion, Denise notes that, as well as these key actors, there are a
number of other forces that influence the construction of school geography,
not least awarding bodies, publishing companies and policy-makers.
However, she also records that certain people within those groups, which she
calls 'elite', have power in influencing how school geography is constructed.
The partisan nature of this model, she concludes, is important to acknowledge. Freeman also reflects on the impact that these findings can have on

practice, not least on the need to have 'conversations' with fellow professionals about the construction of school geography, how it involves young people and how it is represented to them.

Freeman's research is an extremely valuable addition to our understanding of how school geography is constructed. On some levels her results are quite surprising as to how views of individuals can be so influential in the shaping of school geography. It also demonstrates the partisan nature of how school geography is constructed and leads us to consider our own part is sustaining the status quo, or as Freeman suggests, adding our own voices to the conversation about what school geography is, and what it is for.

For discussion

- Consider the content of your geography curriculum. From where has it originated? And whose geography is being constructed? To what extent do the individual teachers and students contribute to the geographical knowledge being taught?
- Some geography teachers find it useful to construct a geographical biography: tracing where your geographical knowledge has come from and what the major influences on it have been. This is also useful to identify gaps, and areas for development. You can critically reflect on how you have maintained your own geographical understanding.
- Consider a recent lesson or scheme of work, and the content therein. Was the geography at the forefront of the learning? To what extent do you emphasise geographical learning over learning?

Further reading

1 *GeogEd*: www.geography.org.uk/projects/gtip/geogede-journal/vol.2issue1 for more information on Freeman's research.
2 Brooks, C. (2006) Geography Teachers and Making the School Geography Curriculum. *Geography*, 91. In this article, Brooks describes three lessons in detail and discusses the geographical content in them and how it could be improved.
3 Lambert, D. (2004) Geography. In White, J. (ed.) *Rethinking the School Curriculum*. Abingdon, RoutledgeFalmer. For further information about the impact of the Original Orders of the Geography National Curriculum.
4 Rawling, E. (2001) *Changing the Subject: the Impact of National Policy on School Geography 1980–2000*. Sheffield, Geographical Association. For more information about the National Curriculum, how it was developed and the influences upon that process.
5 Morgan, J. and Lambert, D. (2005) *Geography: Teaching School Subjects 11–19*. London, Routledge. This book is extremely valuable in placing geographical expertise in context, and exploring its relationship to what happens in classrooms.

References

Allen, J. and Massey, D. (eds) (1995) *Geographical Worlds*. Oxford, Oxford University Press.

Bakan, Joel (2004) *The Corporation: the Pathological Pursuit of Power and Profit*. Robinson Publishing.

Boyer, E.L. (1990) *Scholarship Reconsidered: Priorities of the Professoriate*. Princeton, NJ, Carnegie Foundation for the Advancement of Teaching.

Brooks, C. (2006) Geography Teachers and Making the School Geography Curriculum. *Geography*, 91.

Brooks, C. and Morgan, A. (2006) *Theory into Practice: Cases and Places*. Sheffield, Geographical Association.

Dewey, J. (1972 [1897]) The psychological aspect of the school curriculum. In Boydston, J.A. (ed.) *The Middle Works of John Dewey, 1882–1898* (Vol. 5 1895–1898). Carbondale, IL: Southern Illinios University Press, pp. 164–177.

Dove, J. (1999) *Theory into Practice: Immaculate Misconceptions*. Sheffield, Geographical Association.

Graves, N. (1979) *Curriculum Planning in Geography*. London, Heinemann Educational.

Hutchings, P. and Shulman, L. (1999) The Scholarship of Teaching: New Elaborations, New Developments. *Change*, 31(5), 10–15.

Klein, N. (2001) *No Logo*. Flamingo.

Marsden, W.E. (1997) On Taking the Geography Out of Geographical Education. *Geography*, 82(3).

Massey, D. (1995) Spatial Divisions of Labour: Social Structures and the Geography of Production, 2nd edn. Basingstoke, Macmillan.

Mitchell, D. (ed.) (2009) *Living Geography – Exciting Futures for Teachers and Students*. Cambridge, Chris Kington Publishing.

Morgan, J. and Lambert, D. (2005) *Geography: Teaching School Subjects 11–19*. London, Routledge.

Pring, R. (2007) *John Dewey*. London, Continuum.

Rice, R.E. (1992) Towards a Broader Conception of Scholarship: the American Context. In Whiston, T. and Geiger, R. (eds) *Research and Higher Education: the United Kingdom and the United States*. Buckingham, SRHE/Open University.

Schlosser, E. (2002) *Fast Food Nation*. Penguin

Scott, D. (2008) *Critical Essays on Major Curriculum Theorists*. London: Routledge.

Smith, J.P. and Girod, M. (2003) John Dewey and Psychologizing the Subject-matter: Big Ideas, Ambitious Teaching, and Teacher Education. *Teaching and Teacher Education*, 19, 295–307.

Wellsted, E. (2006) Understanding 'Distant Places'. In Balderstone, D. (ed.) *Secondary Geography Handbook*. Sheffield, Geographical Association.

6 Education for sustainable development and geography education

Alun Morgan

The UNESCO Decade for Education for Sustainable Development (DESD) runs from 2005–2014. This represents an internationally agreed attempt to focus attention on Education for Sustainable Development (ESD) across all educational sectors. In the UK, the most obvious manifestation of a redoubled focus on ESD is the UK Government's 'Sustainable Schools National Framework' for England which is structured around '8 Doorways' to sustainable development. This is being promoted in most schools in England, in both primary and secondary phases. Often the geography specialist is charged with taking a lead role in promoting ESD in school because of the close connection made with the subject in the National Curriculum, and a wider perception in the education community that ESD *is* to do with geography. This is welcomed by many at a time when geography has been losing ground to other subjects as it is hoped that it will make geography more appealing to young people. However, it is a relationship that needs to be approached critically and reflectively. There are dangers as well as benefits in geography tying itself too tightly and uncritically to ESD.

The aims of this chapter are:

- to outline the salient issues related to sustainable development and to discuss the relationship to geographical concepts.
- to consider the various formulations of ESD to support the critical reflection of geography teachers required to negotiate this complex terrain.
- to consider the challenges and opportunities of an inter-disciplinary approach (ESD) to the discipline of geography education.
- to consider the tensions inherent in ESD given both its 'educational' and 'advocacy' dimensions.

What *is* sustainable development?

Before considering '*Education* for Sustainable Development', it is first necessary to consider the 'parent' concept, namely Sustainable Development (SD) and how this relates to 'geography'. This is no simple task, as SD (and consequently ESD) is a contested concept with no single universally agreed definition. Actually the number of definitions currently in use runs into the hundreds, reflecting a spectrum of divergent perspectives! This is compounded by the fact that a similar situation could be said to prevail in the discipline of geography – it is no exaggeration to talk of many geographies being represented in the academy. This is a crucial issue to consider even whilst reading this chapter since, whilst attempting to be objective, the views expressed will necessarily reflect views on SD, ESD and geography held by the author (and must themselves be consequently open to critique!).

However, there are some basic principles that are commonly accepted in all but the most perverse definitions of SD. The seminal and most often quoted definition was presented by the Brundtland Commission, which states that SD 'meets the needs of the present without compromising the ability of future generations to meet their own needs' (WCED 1987). In a nutshell, then, SD is a *normative* concept – it is concerned with creating a *better* world now and in the future, by establishing alternative and better systems and processes for organising human behaviour. This marks it apart from other intellectual pursuits usually associated with academic work, which are usually presented as being objective and value-free, concerned more with describing, understanding and explaining how the world works than prescribing how it *should* work. This distinction is crucial since it lies at the heart of some of the key tensions between geography education and ESD. ESD carries a more overt normative advocacy role (i.e., it is *for* SD) than is felt inappropriate for those who fear this smacks of indoctrination.

Of course, what is considered *better* is highly subjective and dependent on framework and worldview – a capitalist will promote a very different vision for a better world than, for example, a socialist. However, for any vision of a better world to qualify as sustainable development it must consider *both* social *and* environmental systems in a mutually compatible manner. This is reflected in the official title of the Rio Earth Summit in 1992 which popularised the term – the 'United Nations Conference on *Environment and Development*' (UNCED). Thus, SD is concerned with both human systems and natural (biophysical) systems, as well as the *interactions* between them. The emphasis is that neither is compromised but is, instead, developed in a mutually compatible and sustainable manner – hence, sustainable development. UNCED also popularised a conceptual framework of three elements – social, economic and environmental. This framework has been variously schematised as either: three legs of a stool, three overlapping circles (a Venn diagram) or three concentric circles (see Figure 6.1).

This is relatively easy to follow. However, digging a little deeper reveals that each diagram has strengths and weaknesses which reveal some of the inherent complexities of SD. For example, the 'three legs' diagram is useful since it suggests that if any one 'leg' is removed from the equation or consideration, the 'stool' will collapse. Unfortunately, it also suggests that each is relatively discrete and that there are no interactions between them. The Venn diagram is better at revealing the interactions between the elements (the overlapping circles) but also suggests that it is possible to have areas of human

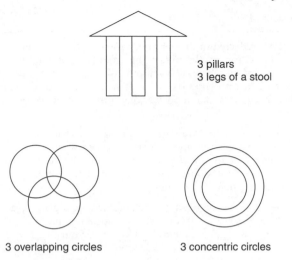

3 pillars
3 legs of a stool

3 overlapping circles   3 concentric circles

Figure 6.1 Three schematic conceptualisations of sustainable development comprising three elements: economic, social and environmental (source: Freeman and Morgan 2009: 31).

action that lie outside, and therefore independently of, either economic, social or environmental systems – you try to think of any that actually do! This problem is addressed in the 'concentric rings' since no element lies outside the others but immediately presents another dilemma – which ring should be the outer one and therefore subsume, or be prioritised over, all the others? For an economist the 'economy' might; for a sociologist, 'society' might; and for an ecologist, 'environment' might.

This is just the tip of the iceberg. The major problem with the seminal Brundtland definition presented above is that it is so broad as to be ambiguous and therefore permits a whole host of divergent interpretations. Furthermore, Scott and Gough (2003: 18–22) identify a range of tensions and paradoxes inherent in the concept of SD itself which permit divergent interpretations based on different ideologies and worldviews. Their analysis is very helpful, not least for unpacking some of the tensions which will necessarily be encountered by geography teachers in their efforts to negotiate (E)SD (see Table 6.1).

What makes SD 'geographical'?

What then makes SD widely recognised as a 'geographical' concept in education? One useful formulation of what constitutes the discipline of 'geography' was presented by Hagget (1983), who suggested that it comprises three inter-dependent elements:

- ecological analysis (or human–environment interactions/relations);
- spatial analysis (pattern and distribution);

Table 6.1 Tensions in the concept of SD

'change versus continuity'	This tension is reflected in the very term used for the concept, since 'sustainable' implies 'keeping things going' and might be 'read' conservatively, whereas 'development' implies 'changing for the better'. A whole host of questions arise as to what is worth conserving or 'sustaining' and what must be changed or 'developed'.
'empowerment versus prescription'	This tension refers to the extent to which people should be supported in making autonomous decisions about what behaviour change (if any!) is required for SD, or whether there is a need for an authority to force people to behave in a certain way given the urgency of the issues.
'me versus we'	This tension concerns the relative merit of encouraging action at the individual or collective level. Generally speaking, more liberal and right-wing perspectives are likely to favour the former, whereas more socialist ones will prefer the latter.
'present generations versus future generations'	This tension asks whether efforts should be focused on improving the lot of people today (through promoting social justice and equity) or on ensuring that the generations to come inherit a world at least as good as the one we now occupy (e.g. through the preservation of biodiversity and conservation of resources, possibly at the expense of present generations).
'humans versus nature'	This tension concerns whether or not efforts should be *anthropocentric* (focused largely on the human world, e.g. promoting social justice and human rights even if these might result in damage to biodiversity); or more *eco-/bio-centric* (focused on the natural world even if people suffer as a result).
'local versus global'	This tension questions the most appropriate scale for action – an inherently geographical tension. Is it enough to 'Think Global but Act Local'? Or do we need to simultaneously act across a range of scales?
'rich, poor and very poor'	This tension relates to 'social justice'. Should the focus be on punishing and/or changing the behaviour and even the very economic system of those largely responsible for *un*sustainable development (the 'rich' whether at the individual or international, i.e. MEDC, level)? Or should the focus be on using their accumulated wealth and 'the market' to support those most vulnerable (the very poor)?
'disconnected lumps of joined-up thinking'	This tension implies that SD is an inherently complex concept that requires *both* analysis *and* synthesis. This is a crucial tension in terms of educational debates because it requires a careful consideration of the tension between advocates of disciplinary specialisation (such as geography) which can provide analytical frameworks versus cross-curricular or inter-disciplinary approaches (such as ESD) which are perceived to be better at synthesis. Many would argue that geography is already good at both analysis and synthesis – hence its relevance as a vehicle for ESD.

Source: Scott and Gough 2003.

- complex regional synthesis (which combines/integrates the two other approaches).

Arguably, all three facets are relevant to SD. SD *is* a matter of human–environment interactions and therefore it is crucial to understand both to make appropriate decisions. Similarly, the systems and processes implicated in sustainable development are distributed spatially, and interact through complex spatial relations, therefore spatial analysis is also important to SD. Finally, academic practices can be seen as reductive in that they only focus on individual 'pieces' of the puzzle. SD calls for synthesis to arrive at a holistic account and understanding of the issue at hand – Hagget's third facet of geography.

Turning to a more recent formulation, Whitehead (2007) has provided an excellent introduction to the 'geographies of sustainability'. He suggests that 'thinking geographically' about sustainability issues involves three dimensions or 'lenses' which bear comparison to Hagget's facets. Whitehead's account reflects more 'contemporary' or postmodern developments in the field of geography:

- *Space* (or *thinking 'spatially'*) – Whitehead insists that we need to consider how causes and effects are not evenly distributed across the globe; and, just as importantly, how the issues themselves are perceived differently in different places such as 'the West' or in 'post-socialist states'.
- *Integration* (or providing *integrated accounts*) – for instance, providing a holistic account of the phenomenon under consideration which integrates economic, social and environmental factors (the 'three legs of the sustainability stool').
- *Scale* – understood not as discrete hierarchical ordering of space but as a *relational* category which reveals 'the ways in which global processes are intertwined with processes operating in states, regions, cities, communities and homes' (2007: 27).

Furthermore, Whitehead suggests that 'thinking geographically' about sustainability issues is important since it 'helps to reveal the constructed nature of sustainability and uncover alternative sustainabilities or *countercurrents* to sustainable development' (2007: 26), precisely what is needed for critically reflective professional development.

SD discourses and typologies

The above section reveals that there are a great variety of sometimes divergent perspectives encapsulated by the umbrella term 'sustainable development' which reflect different ideologies and worldviews. To unpack this complexity, some authors have attempted to create *typologies* – analytical frameworks to tease apart 'types' of perspectives that share a range of assumptions and prescriptions. Some are relatively simple, such as dividing the 'types' along traditional 'left/socialist–centre/liberal–right/conservative' political lines (see, for example, Dobson 1990). Another relatively simple approach adopted by authors such as O'Riordan (1989) and Fien (1995) is to dichotomise perspectives into *either* anthropocentric (focused on the human realm) *or* ecocentric (focused on 'nature'). Sometimes this simple binary is further dichotomised, giving rise to four positions. A more sophisticated approach has been adopted by Dryzek (2005) who adopts a 'discourse approach' through which he derives a new typology involving as many as nine perspectives.

   Whilst helpful as analytical frameworks, one must approach such typologies with caution. Typologies that 'split' or dichotomise the range of perspectives into binaries are deceptively simple. On the other hand, the more sophisticated the typology, the more it becomes unwieldy. An additional shortcoming of many such typologies is that they are often presented as objective descriptors, whereas they invariably carry a normative message, tending to implicitly 'privilege' a particular position, usually the more radical one. For example, both Dobson and Dryzek's typologies reflect their preferred ideological position. However, when read with a critical eye, these typologies can be a useful tool to analyse sustainable practices.

Education *for* sustainable development – what's in a label?

Having looked at a variety of perspectives on SD, it is now appropriate to turn our attention more specifically towards the response of the educational community. Much of the preceding discussion about tensions and different perspectives within SD is, unsurprisingly, recapitulated in Education for Sustainable Development debates. Consequently, a variety of perspectives exist within the educational community (and within the geography education community) in terms of SD. This section attempts to chart two of these different perspectives.[1] Of course, the cautions about using labels and typologies highlighted above must be constantly borne in mind!

Environmental education and development education

The first crucial distinction pertinent to ESD debates is the relative focus on environmental vis-à-vis development issues. In many ways this reflects two key antecedents to ESD: Environmental Education (EE) and Development Education (DE). Both had their origins in the 1970s as educational responses to a variety of issues that were then becoming apparent. Environmental Education was particularly concerned with environmental issues such as loss of habitat, species extinction, pollution etc. Environmental organisations such as WWF were key proponents. Developmental Education, on the other hand, was more 'human-centred', being focused on issues such as poverty reduction and social justice. DE was strongly supported by charities such as Oxfam (see

Chapter 4). Into the 1980s, a number of authors identified significant overlap between the respective issues and started to make common cause between environmental and development education (e.g. Grieg *et al.* 1987, 1989). This was occurring about the same time (and for the same reasons) as debates were shifting towards SD as an integrative concept in non-educational circles. It was natural, therefore, for a new term – Education for Sustainable Development (ESD) – to be coined to convey this integration of environmental and development education, with the proviso that the new approach to education would be 'more than the sum of these parts'. Alternative integrative terms were also being coined around this time, such as 'World Studies' and 'Global Education'.

ESD *should* be interpreted as being concerned with *both* environmental *and* development issues. However, it is apparent that many approaches that speak of ESD remain strongly and narrowly associated with one or other of the two 'camps' or traditions – environmental *or* development. Furthermore, it is often the case that ESD is narrowly interpreted as being a reformulation of environment education, with the consequence that developmental or social-justice dimensions are often downplayed or even missing. It is a constant battle to redress this imbalance. Some have taken to spelling out the 'missing dimension' by using the rather unwieldy and tautological phrase 'Education for Sustainable Development and Global Citizenship' (ESDGC), since the latter part – Global Citizenship – is more strongly associated with development education. This is the approach adopted in Wales and by the UK Network for Initial Teacher Education. The relative balance of environmental to development issues addressed in ESD and geography education must, therefore, be constantly borne in mind.

Education for sustainable development versus education for sustainability

Another contentious issue relates to the desirability or otherwise of the term 'Sustainable Development'. For many, the term is acceptable and broad enough to allow for multiple perspectives to be included. For others (e.g. Wade 2008) Sustainable Development, and the word 'development' in particular, is too closely associated with a Western, neo-liberal capitalist ideology or a model of development that is perceived to be the root of the problem. As a consequence, they are more likely to prefer to use the term 'Education for Sustainability' (EFS) to distinguish the kind of education called for. Whilst in sympathy with this argument, this chapter uses the term 'ESD' since it is perceived to be broad enough to encompass all perspectives and understandings (capitalist *and* anti-capitalist, and all positions in between); and, second, because it is the preferred term in the UK and international (e.g. United Nations) contexts.

Geography education versus ESD

Having set out a range of perspectives and approaches to ESD, it is now appropriate in this final section to turn our attention to understanding the relationship between ESD and geography education. Actually, this task must be ultimately left to you as practitioner-researcher since each member of the geography-education community must come to their own critically reflective and authentic position on the relationship between ESD and geography education. This is a crucial professional task. Consequently, this final section will highlight some of the areas to be tackled; and present some examples of how others have done so.

A great many geography educators are happy that ESD is being tied so closely to their subject, partly for the marketing and recruitment reasons alluded to above, but also from a desire to promote, through education and their subject, a 'better world'. Indeed, a great many have chosen to teach geography precisely because it represents a primary vehicle for exploring environmental and development issues. Conversely, there are those who are very worried about the close connection being made between the subject and ESD. Either perspective is understandable and acceptable. However, it is incumbent on practitioners to dig a little deeper and to explore critically and reflectively the educational implications of such a personal position. A key task is to listen, and respond, to critical voices from other perspectives. Since the case has already been forcefully made *for* a strong relationship between geography and ESD in the curriculum, the focus of this section will be on those arguments urging caution if not a wholesale rejection of such a close connection. Critiques of too close a relationship between ESD and geography education can be discerned in terms of two distinctive problems: its interdisciplinary nature and advocatory purpose.

ESD is not a single subject but rather an inter- or trans-disciplinary *approach* to education. It is likely to draw strongly on science, geography and technology, but actually all subjects are perceived to have a strong contribution to make. Furthermore, the focus is as much on process as content. In this respect it resembles other educational formulations which transcend disciplines such as 'social studies'. Critics of such cross-curricular approach decry the lack of disciplinary rigour and identity. 'Disciplined' knowledge, from such a perspective, provides appropriate training in the conceptual frameworks, criteria and skills that can fruitfully be applied to a problem or issue. Approaches drawing on a range of approaches, without a sound grounding in any, can result in superficiality and run the risk that misconceptions, inaccurate knowledge and received wisdom will be accidentally promulgated and not challenged. Furthermore, disciplines have staying power and efficacy because they have developed over time through the collective efforts of legions of workers inducted into the traditions of the discipline. This tried-and-tested disciplinary tradition provides a check against mere 'bandwagon jumping' of the latest 'societal fad' which might compromise the integrity of the discipline. Perhaps SD (and the associated environmental and development issues) is merely another such 'bandwagon' which could compromise this very integrity for the sake of 'political correctness'?

An alternative yet related critique concerns the advocatory and instrumental nature of ESD – it is supposed to be education *for* something – which could smack of indoctrination. Actually, all education must surely be *for* something; that is, have an 'instrumental' purpose. Of course, it is possible to make a distinction between different instrumentalities. The narrowest form of educational instrumentalism is usually considered to be 'economic instrumentalism' which sees the end point of education as serving the needs of the labour market through training for work. 'Autonomous instrumentalism', in contrast, sees the end goal of education as being the development of autonomous, fully developed human beings capable of making up their own minds. 'Critical instrumentalism' in contrast is concerned with equipping society with the knowledge, skills, attitudes and values required to change society for the better. It would seem to be that the crucial tension therefore is between those who subscribe to 'autonomous instrumentalist' educational ideology (which supports individual 'enlightenment' and independence) and those that subscribe to a 'critical instrumentalist one' who wish to promote 'societal transformation'. Perhaps these two instrumentalities can, and indeed should, be resolved in good ESD and geographical education.

Geography educators respond

The contentious relationship between ESD and geography education represents a fruitful field for educational research since it represents a complex 'issue of concern' for the geography-education community. Some practitioner-researchers are sceptical and devote their efforts to arguing against a close relationship (see Standish's writing under 'Further reading', page 87). More typically, the terrain is explored by geography educators who are advocates of linking ESD and geography to a greater or lesser extent. Typically, the following sequence is followed:

1 Reviewing the field and range of possible definitions and formulations of ESD and/or ESD-geography education relations.
2 Selecting, or establishing, a personally appropriate definition and formulation of ESD-geography education.
3 Defending their particular interpretation of ESD(-geography education).
4 Putting this interpretation 'to work' either in the design, application and/or evaluation of an educational programme (for example, a scheme of work), an existing programme (such as the National Curriculum or an examination syllabus), or an educational approach (such as 'enquiry-based' learning) in the light of this perspective.
5 Identifying recommendations and further challenges

Such an approach has been fruitfully adopted at Masters level for both modular assignments and dissertations. For example, in her module assignment Downes (2005) first defined ESD and identified key challenges. She then went on to demonstrate that geography can take a key leadership role in inter-disci-plinary teaching. Finally she evaluated positively the 'enquiry approach' for teaching sustainability. Similarly, Moody (2005) sought to evaluate the extent to which the AQA GCSE syllabus permitted the teaching of sustainability as advocated in the literature. After reviewing what is meant by sustainability and ESD, she went on to consider whether or not the form of ESD she identified in the literature could be achieved within the prevailing 'educational paradigm', considering in particular the potential role of geography. Finally, she taught and evaluated a series of five GCSE lessons following the AQA syllabus, concluding that the syllabus was too constrained, both in terms of time allocation and com-plexity of issues explored, to provide a truly meaningful vehicle for ESD. Davis (2005) also wished to explore the potential for teaching ESD through a GCSE syllabus. Once again, he first set out his 'frame of reference' but this time rather than extensively reviewing the literature, he providing an account of the eco-centric perspective – deep ecology – he was concerned to explore as a possible vehicle for ESD-geography education. He then presented and justified a sequence of lessons that were taught and evaluated.

Dissertation summary

Baughen, Bernadette (2006) 'Global Citizenship in Initial Teacher Training: an Exploration of Trainee's Thinking'

Baughen's dissertation took a different approach to the coursework described above, partly reflecting the length of her work; but also because of her unique position as a teacher–educator rather than classroom practitioner. Her disser-tation reveals that labels are sometimes interchangeable since she uses the term 'Global Citizenship' throughout rather than 'ESD', but the latter term could have been substituted for the former virtually without consequence. Her first section represented an extensive literature review that explored the field of Global Citizenship. Then she presented her primary research, which was into the attitudes of student teachers (trainee primary teachers in the first year of a four-year BEd course) towards global issues prior to and then after their undertaking a short module in Global Citizenship. It should be noted that these trainees are not geography specialists, but Baughen framed the course in terms of geography. She employed a variety of research methods to elicit her data, including questionnaires and group interviews. Baughen was able to conclude that 'a short intensive programme surrounding key aspects of global citizenship achieved a level of success in helping to clarify trainees' thinking, and to contribute to their professional and personal development' (2006: 84). In particular, trainees expressed a consequent 'commitment to the notion of personal reflection and critical thinking in the classroom' (2006: 86). Yet Baughen also discerned that trainees expressed concerns 'in terms of the skills required on the part of the teacher to enable this to happen'. Consequently, she recommended that this lack of confidence represents a key area to be addressed in initial teacher education (ITE), but also acknowledged that this represents a challenge given the already crowded ITE curriculum.

For discussion

Consider your professional practice in the light of the following questions:

*   Thinking particularly about environmental and/or development issues you teach, is it ever right to 'teach' what is 'right' and 'wrong'?
*   What do you consider your professional role in society to be in relation to SD?
*   Which 'version', if any, of ESD described in this chapter would you be happy to subscribe to and promote through your geography teaching?
*   How would you respond to a call in your school to teach SD as a cross-curricular theme?
*   What aspects of the existing geography curriculum could be changed (perhaps reduced/removed or foregrounded more explicitly) to provide more scope for ESD without compromising the geography?

Further reading

1 Morgan, A. (2006) Sustainable development and global citizenship: the 'new agenda' for geographical education in England and Wales, in Chi-kin Lee, J. and Williams, M. (eds) (2006) *Environmental and Geographical Education for Sustainability*. New York: Nova Science Publisher Inc. For an account of the historical development of ESD in the UK.
2 Reid, A. (2000) Environmental change and sustainable development, in Grimwade, K. (ed.) *Geography and the New Agenda*. Sheffield: Geographical Association. For a critical discussion of the relationship between ESD and geography.
3 Morgan, J. and Lambert, D. (2005) *Teaching School Subjects: Geography, Teaching School Subjects 11–19*. London: RoutledgeFalmer; Standish, A. (2007) Geography used to be about maps. In *The Corruption of the Curriculum*. R. Whelan (ed.). London: Civitas; Standish, A. (2008) *Global Perspectives in the Geography Curriculum: Reviewing the Moral Case for Geography*. London: Routledge. For arguments in favour of geography education's need to remain cautious and independent of 'fashionable' and value-laden educational projects such as environmentalism, development issues, sustainable development etc.

Note

1 Readers who are interested in other typologies should also read: Huckle and Sterling (1996); Agyeman (2005); Agyeman and Evans (2004); Scott and Gough (2004); and Vare and Scott (2007).

References

Agyeman, J. (2005) *Sustainable Communities and the Challenge of Environmental Justice*. New York: New York University Press.

Agyeman, J. and B. Evans (2004) 'Just sustainability': the emerging discourse of environmental justice in Britain? *The Geographical Journal* 170(2): 155–164.

Davis, N. (2005) *The use of different perspectives in teaching GCSE Environmental Management – with special emphasis on the 'Deep Ecology' perspective*. Module assignment submitted in part fulfilment of the MA in Geography in Education at the Institute of Education, University of London.

Dobson, A. (1990) *Green Political Thought: an Introduction*. London: Unwin Hyman.

Downes, K. (2005) *The benefits and problems of teaching sustainable development at Key Stage 3: is geographical enquiry a possible solution?* Module assignment submitted in part fulfilment of the MA in Geography in Education at the Institute of Education, University of London.

Dryzek, J.S. (2005) *The Politics of the Earth: Environmental Discourses*. 2nd edn. Oxford: Oxford University Press.

Fien, J. (1995) Ideology: orientation in environmentalism. In *Education for the Environment: Critical Curriculum Theorising and Environmental Education*. J. Fien (ed.). Geelong: Deakin University Press, pp. 23–29.

Freeman, D. and Morgan, A. (2009) Living in the future–education for sustainable development. In *Living Geography*. D. Mitchell (ed.). London, Chris Kington Publishing.

Grieg, S., G. Pike and D. Selby (1987) *Earthrights: Education as if the Planet Really Mattered*. London: The World Wide Fund/Kogan Page.

Grieg, S., G. Pike and D. Selby (1989) *Green Prints for Changing Schools*. London: The World Wide Fund/Kogan Page.

Hagget, P. (1983) *Geography: a Modern Synthesis*. 3 edn. New York: Harper & Row.

Huckle, J. and Sterling, S. (eds) (1996) *Education for Sustainability*. London: Earthscan.

Moody, A. (2005) *An evaluation of a series of lessons on sustainability in the light of recent literature and the GCSE syllabus*. Module assignment submitted in part fulfilment of the MA in Geography in Education at the Institute of Education, University of London.

O'Riordan, T. (1989) The challenge for environmentalism. In *New Models in Geography*. R. Peet and N. Thrift (eds). Boston: Unwin Hyman, pp. 77–102.

Scott, W. and S. Gough (2003) *Sustainable Development and Learning: Framing the Issues*. London: RoutledgeFalmer.

Scott, W. and S. Gough (2004) *Key Issues in Sustainable Development and Learning: a Critical Review*. London: RoutledgeFalmer.

Vare, P. and W. Scott (2007) Learning for a change: exploring the relationship between education and sustainable development. *Journal for Education for Sustainable Development* 1(2): 191–198.

Wade, R. (2008) Journeys around sustainability: mapping the terrain. In *Journeys Around Education for Sustainability*. J. Parker and R. Wade (eds). London: LSBU.

WCED (1987) *Our Common Future (The Brundtland Report)*. Oxford: Oxford University Press.

Whitehead, M. (2007) *Spaces of Sustainability: Geographical Perspectives on the Sustainable Society*. Abingdon: Routledge.

7 Being critical when teaching with technologies

David Mitchell

This chapter aims to critically examine the role of information and communication technologies (ICTs), particularly geographical information systems (GIS) in the school geography curriculum.

The aims of this chapter are:

• to identify the rationales for using GIS and ICTs in school geography.
• to explore the theory behind these rationales.
• to show how geography teachers have used theory in their classroom practice with GIS and ICTs.

Is ICT important for geography teaching?

Familiarity with the Internet has become such that 'to Google' has become almost synonymous with 'to learn' in the popular imagination (Lidstone and Stoltman 2006). Most young people in the developed world want to be connected with other people and places at all times, through text messaging, email and Internet spaces (Robertson and Fluck 2004). So, this pervasion of technology, and young people's enjoyment of it, may seem justification enough to embrace technologies in the classroom and the field. Further justification for ICT use comes from the argument that schools must develop work-related, generalised skills. ICT's role here is to motivate the learner, give access to material or to help organise and present their thinking. This is the 'learning to learn' rationale or 'pedagogic adventure' (Morgan and Lambert 2005). A rationale for using ICT based on these arguments neglects a subject-based rationale. Geographic information and ICT in the classroom can be seen not only in these subject-free ways, but there is a case for a *geographical* basis, underpinned by theory, for using new technologies in school geography. This chapter, therefore, makes a case for GIS (and other ICTs) in school geography, but stresses the importance of a theoretically informed rationale for their adoption. Before moving on to a specifically geographical rationale for ICTs, it is useful to expand on the generic or cross-curricular rationale for ICTs in the schooling of young people.

A generic rationale for teaching with ICTs

Motivation

The motivation of pupils, including differentiation and inclusion advantages, is, in practice, the most popular (and often the only) justification by teachers for using ICTs to teach and learn geography. Reports from Ofsted (2008) and BECTA (2004) also emphasise this, but as Ofsted note, more enjoyment does not always mean more learning: 'Although pupils enjoy using ICT, too often the work involves no more than mundane searches of the internet with little thinking about the geography' (Ofsted 2008: 12).

It is obvious from teacher evaluation of lessons that ICT can alter the classroom atmosphere to striking effect, often in positive ways, bringing pupils on task, raising interest and concentration levels.

A motivation rationale for using ICTs can be underpinned by theory in three distinct ways. The first is multiple intelligence (MI) theory (Gardner 1983). MI theory has been hugely influential in the classroom, leading to efforts by teachers to vary their range of 'learning styles' and assessment strategies. ICT is very useful to this end, allowing, in particular, much visual–spatial learning. The second useful theory is that of stimulating 'situational interest' (Hidi and Ainley 2002). This argues that the use of ICT itself can interest students, regardless of what is taught. Psychological theories of motivation, including those of situational and individual interest theory (Hidi and Ainley 2002), may be used to support using ICT as a hook for pupils and a 'way in' to the development of interest in and enjoyment of learning a school subject. The third useful theory is that ICTs tap into 'young people's worlds' (Holloway and Valentine 2000; Skelton and Valentine 1998). For instance, the 'Young People's Geography project' (Firth and Biddulph 2009) explores young people's thinking and preferred ways of learning. Students learn online by trial and error, going back and forth from one transient screen of information to the next – distinctly different from patiently reading pages in a book. Young people often *prefer* to communicate and learn with ICT.

The vocational argument

The second rationale for using ICTs and GIS is often focused on the development of workplace skills. The use of technology can support 'soft skills' such as team-working, problem-solving and encourage positive attitudes to learning. In addition, it is often cited that industry needs a supply of school leavers with ICT skills, including specific GIS skills and understanding, for the growing GIS industry.

The 'soft-skills' rationale for ICT is rather tenuous (in that a range of non–ICT media or resources could also be argued to support such skills), but popular amongst teachers; for example, GIS is seen as an ideal tool to support a project-management approach to investigate fieldwork (Mitchell 2009). There is a stronger argument to support the second rationale – that GIS in school will directly support young people in finding jobs in the GIS industry.

Bednarz (2001) explores what she summarises as the 'workplace justification'– that skills are needed to compete in a changing global economy of 'knowledge workers' capable of using 'decision support systems' such as GIS to handle and analyse growing amounts of data. This argument has often been cited by those who place emphasis on knowledge workers as playing a key role in competitiveness in a modern globalised world. However, Bednarz contests these assumptions, arguing that this prediction of the future job market is problematic. The idea that the economy needs 'knowledge workers' and the meaning of a 'knowledge' or 'digital' economy is contested by others, for example by Lambert and Morgan (2009). Morgan suggests there are unfounded assumptions of technological determinism being made, and argues that technology does not necessarily drive innovation and economic development. Issues of environmental sustainability and social cohesion, for instance, are under-represented by those who cite an all-pervading, globalised 'knowledge economy'.

Bednarz also urges caution in adopting the workplace rationale, on the basis that it neglects the purpose of education:

> While providing students with key technological skills is a worthwhile and legitimate concern of education, geography educators should be cautious about serving a merely essentialist role providing trained knowledge workers for the Information Economy as opposed to preparing educated spatially skilled individuals.
>
> (2001: 3)

This alert to the problematic nature of this justification for using GIS does not negate it completely. For some young people, the most tangible reason for using GIS may be the GIS career they aspire to. Furthermore, skills developed with GIS are also relevant to geography in higher education. GIS courses, both within geography degrees and as separate degrees in their own right, have grown. Graduates with GIS skills are highly employable in a range of sectors. Lambert's discussion of 'geo-capability' (2008) reminds us of the role of GIS as preparation for future work and life.

Geographical rationales

The next section explores the geographical arguments for teaching with ICTs and GIS, and proposes four distinct rationales for their use in education. First, GIS can be seen as a process or mechanism that can in itself change people and places (critical GIS and participatory GIS). Second, GIS can support learning to think spatially, and thus the broader idea of 'thinking geographically'. Third, GIS can enable accurate and precise data gathering and analysis, for rigorous geographical enquiry. Fourth and finally, with the arrival of the Internet and 'cyberspace', new technologies have created virtual spaces and places – the study of which falls within the scope of geography.

Critical and participatory GIS

Both critical and participatory GIS consider the effect GIS has on people and places. In doing so, they share a distinctly geographical approach to the outcomes of using GIS. Critical GIS sees the use of GIS packages to process data as a process and not as value free. This process affects people, places and how we see the world, hence it becomes of central interest to geography. GIS is constructed socially, designed in a value-laden world in which the purpose and use of the software cannot be ignored. For example, the 'science wars' in the early 1990s were instrumental in the development of GIS. GIS was used to control or mediate global defence systems. More recently, conclusions about people and places drawn from data using a GIS are often seen as objective and value free. However, Schuurman (2000) has highlighted a 'methodological chasm' between GIS software developers and the human geographers beginning to look at the effects of this technology. Schuurman and Pratt (2002) take a feminist perspective on GIS, arguing that the software can have specific outcomes for women and that women have specific gains to make from more involvement with GIS. Sieber (2000) agrees that GIS can be a valuable tool if used by social movements.

This perspective of GIS as a social tool is developed further in participatory GIS (or PGIS). PGIS goes beyond looking at the effect of GIS on the world and suggests that widening participation can democratise GIS. The aim of PGIS is to encourage inclusion in the GIS process, thereby broadening the base of those in control of knowledge production. The emphasis is on enabling people to use GIS at a local level, to represent their local area the way they see it. PGIS can be thought of as a shift from a technological drive – *GIS because it is possible* – to a more social one – *GIS because it is needed* (Fargher 2008). This approach also challenges the power structures that have tended to dominate the GIS process. PGIS, although far from unproblematic – power and access to the mapping will never be equal to all – has much potential for school geography. For example, it is being used with London schools through the open Internet-based mapping of the charity London 21.

School geography can also explore GIS as a geographical phenomenon. If the focus is on learning *with* GIS, pupils might focus on a geographical question, such as 'how is my local town structured?' and make use of the GIS, without necessarily needing to think through or reflect on the GIS itself. But critical GIS theory and participatory GIS suggest that, at some point, such an investigation should also consider *what* a GIS is, how it operates and for what purpose. Learning *about* GIS is challenging for teachers and learners, as it takes them beyond passive learning. O'Connor (2007) suggests there are three levels:

- presenting spatial data;
- processing and analysing spatial data;
- data input and editing of spatial data.

This progression may be helpful for teachers and pupils struggling to differentiate between software (i.e. from *Google Earth* to *ArcGIS*). Understanding the GIS process means that students can question when it is appropriate to use GIS selectively, thereby preventing them from overusing it, simply because it exists.

Learning to think spatially

There has been much concern (particularly in the USA) about how school geography supports the spatial element of the discipline, and GIS has been heralded by some as the future for pupils' 'spatial thinking'. Bednarz (2001) discusses an 'educative justification' for using GIS, i.e. that using GIS supports the teaching and learning of geography. The functioning of a GIS mirrors the spatial thinking processes of the brain. Bednarz points to the three dimensions of spatial thinking – spatial visualisation, spatial orientation and spatial relations, as outlined by Golledge and Stimson (1997). Spatial relations are most commonly developed in geography classrooms and include, amongst others, recognising spatial distributions and spatial patterns, connecting locations, sketch mapping and comparing maps. Essentially, the argument is that, by using a GIS, students are *practising* and so improving their spatial relational skills. It is a neat and attractive argument, but Bednarz concedes, 'While it seems intuitive that GIS will compliment the development of key geographic skills it is not yet proven' (Bednarz 2001: 2).

Bednarz takes the educative justification a step further by suggesting that, by closely mirroring processes in the brain of 'cognitive mapping', a GIS may support reasoning and problem–solving beyond spatial and geographical terms. For example, by 'mapping out' problems in our heads, we practise thinking spatially, and become better in *all* problem solving. The implication is that we must be capable of spatialising the non-spatial. For instance we may represent non-spatial phenomena like temperature and time on a graph, laying them out spatially.

Bednarz's work is reflected in the findings of a substantial research project into spatial thinking carried out in the USA by the National Research Council (NRC 2006). The NRC also suggests that the user of a GIS is practising, and improving, their spatial thinking. The NRC argues, however, that the three elements to spatial thinking are rather different to the spatial visualisation, orientation and relations identified by Golledge and Stimson (1997). Rather, the NRC classify them as:

- concepts of space;
- tools of representation;
- processes of reasoning.

The report suggests that these three elements can be both internalised (i.e. operated in our mind) or externalised, in the operation of a GIS, or even on a piece of paper.

Space as a conceptual and analytical framework is familiar to geographers. The second element 'tools of representation' focuses on GIS as a tool supporting a range of ways to manipulate data, and re-present it. GIS enables complex operations like transformations of scale (by zooming in and out), changes of perspective and rotation, measurements of distance and direction, adding layers of data to the same location, symbolising data and attributing further data to existing data. These manipulations can reflect the nature of the data itself or its presentation. The third element, 'process of reasoning', makes sense of the combination of both concepts of space and tools of representation. The computational power of GIS facilitates the operation of queries, thereby facilitating this process of reasoning.

The approaches to justifying GIS through spatial thinking, discussed by the NRC and Bednarz, take a psychological and even neurological theoretical standpoint. Gersmehl and Gersmehl (2006) explore the neurological grounding for spatial thinking, and argue there is a distinct set of spatial-thinking skills, developed from neurological science:

• comparison
• aura (similar to sphere of influence)
• region
• hierarchy
• transition
• analogy
• pattern
• association.

The neurological approach to understanding spatial thinking may not sit easily with social-constructivist views of geographical learning. Further, it may not be wise to overstate the spatial skills, or indeed the position of geography as some sort of spatial science. The discipline is far broader than this. The NRC suggest caution:

> There is as yet no clear consensus about spatial thinking and, therefore, spatial literacy. Thus, there are many related concepts in use: we speak about spatial ability, spatial reasoning, spatial cognition, spatial concepts, spatial intelligence, environmental cognition, cognitive mapping, and mental maps.
>
> (2006: 26)

However, close attention to what, exactly, is being learned when pupils are 'thinking spatially' may enrich geography lessons and challenge pupils. Geographers are familiar with many of the spatial concepts, such as pattern, region, sphere of influence (aura) association (of a certain condition or feature with another condition) and transition (from one type of condition to another). However, these concepts are rarely made explicit to school pupils.

There could be much to gain from making them more explicit in lessons. The concepts can be simply used, for instance, as prompts for thinking – a means to encourage the articulation of spatial thinking through the use of spatial language. Spatial thinking, although complex, challenging and contested, should not be ignored by the geography teacher rationalising the use of GIS for learning.

Accuracy and precision

A further, distinct rationale for GIS is that of precision and accuracy in data and its analysis. Rigorous geographical enquiry requires accessing and producing accurate and precise data and analysis (Roberts 2003). Accuracy and precision are not the essence of all geographical learning, but they are valuable. GIS makes an important contribution here both as a flexible tool and, with digital GI, a source of current data. Wiegand (2006) and Martin (2006) demonstrate how accurate and critical mapping with GIS can be used in the classroom. For example, GCSE pupils can challenge the Burgess model of urban land use with real census data. Using geographical information gives pupils the opportunity to investigate real places, to make an informed judgement, accepting or rejecting a theory, based on accurate and precise data collection and analysis.

Virtual spaces and places

The Internet has created new virtual spaces and places. Young people often inhabit these virtual places, and geography is the school subject best positioned to enable them to deepen their understanding of cyberspace as places and spaces. This has the added advantage of connecting with young people's worlds. Virtual spaces can be seen as free from political control, not limited by bodily location, wealth or identity, and so they may provide more equitable access and have a democratising influence on society.

In his essay for part-completion of the MA in Geography Education, Cassidy (2005) draws on such theory. He asks whether geography teachers should be teaching about virtual place and space within geography and suggests a number of ways in which it might be practically applied in the classroom. He maps his own virtual networks (such as Facebook-type 'friends' and other online communications) in real space, finding distinct spatial patterns that stretch across the globe. Cassidy argues this challenges the viewpoint that cyberspace has no inherent geography of place. He also challenges the idea that cyberspace is a democratising influence, as access to it is far from equal between groups of people.

These four geographical rationales, and the generic rationales for using GIS and ICTs discussed earlier, help to frame thinking about how and why you might use ICT and GIS in your teaching. As you read the dissertation summary that illustrates them, you may like to reflect on these questions:

1   What do you understand by GIS?
2   How does theory and research help to develop a rationale for using ICT?
3   How do pupils 'think spatially' in their geography lessons?

Dissertation summary

Mary Fargher (2004) 'An Investigation into the Effectiveness of GIS to Enhance Spatial Skills in Enquiry-Based Learning'

Fargher's dissertation is chosen to illustrate this chapter as she both critically assesses the development of spatial skills in her use of GIS, and considers other justifications for using GIS with pupils.

Fargher sets out with a clear understanding of what she is looking for in GIS use. She is interested in the spatial skills used, developed and acquired by her students as they undertake a geographical enquiry on the extent that the Titanic disaster in 1912 was natural. The enquiry was originally designed by Joseph Kerski as a means of applying GIS to geographical learning, and it is broken into a series of questions on the ship's course, location, ocean currents, sea depth, influence of the continental shelf and so on.

Fargher's literature review focuses on the debates about *what* spatial skills are (a contested area) and she draws on Bednarz (2001), Golledge and Stimpson (1997) and Kerski (2003) to begin to identify which ones she will be looking for in the classroom. An interesting way in which she further combines research and practice is her design of a rubric for assessing pupils' attainment, and development, of spatial skills. She combines the Geography GCSE specifications for her class with the original rubric designed by Kerski to produce a table of five levels of GIS mastery to think spatially.

Fargher concludes that the use of GIS has supported spatial skills for many students, particularly in visualisation, locational understanding, map projection (spatial orientation), and understanding scale. Importantly, she remains critically evaluative, however, and accepts that she is unable to tie in some of the suggested advantages of using a GIS from her literature review. For example, Bednarz (2001) argues that GIS may support problem solving by mirroring the 'cognitive mapping' processes in the brain – a difficult thing to show from classroom observation. Fargher also concludes that the GIS has supported learning in ways other than just spatial-skill development, including the 'resource-rich' nature of the learning platform that GIS provided – describing this as a 'technical one stop shop for geography'. She also notes the level of challenge and rigour that GIS supported by providing this resource-rich and multi-faceted approach to geographical enquiry. Further, she finds motivation was apparently increased with the use of GIS. The speed at which students could handle data enabled them to get to higher-order analysis. This last point about pace is a good example of how Mary's practice has been influenced by her reading of research. She is interested in the way GIS could change pupils' enquiry by speeding up their handling of complex data.

Whilst engaging with an enquiry using GIS with students, Audet (1993) describes an encounter with one student who appeared to be rapidly rattling through the menus of ArcView. Thinking the student was clearly off task he asked him to stop hitting the keys so quickly and asked him why he was doing this at all, to which the boy replied: 'that's the way I learn' (Audet 1993).

(Fargher 2004: 69)

Fargher found a raised awareness of the use of GIS and spatial skills in the workplace – students wanted to know more about real-world applications of GIS. These latter points were not part of the original research aim (to isolate spatial skills within the use of GIS) but, given that the approach was action research, it was valid to draw out these findings. Finally, Fargher is very aware of the limitations to her case-study approach, and she is wary of making generalisations, assumptions and focusing overly on the advantages of GIS, being a self-professed advocate of their use. It is impossible to remain completely unbiased when involved in one's own practitioner research, but it is important to resist the temptation to make convenient assumptions that can become a 'sales pitch' for the approach you support.

For discussion

- Uncovering the thinking processes behind students using ICT, and the spatial-thinking processes specifically in students using GIS, is important for geography teachers, which remains relatively under researched. Gershmehl and Gershmehl's classification of spatial-thinking processes (2006) provides scope for their identification, which can support student learning with GIS. Research into space and how spatial understanding is constructed by Massey (2005) takes a more sociological perspective, but could also be useful background for investigating how GIS is supporting students' development of concepts of space and how space and place is represented to them.
- The role of GIS as a skill for future life and work is an important area for research. Ideas of 'geographic capability' (Lambert 2008) 'thinking geographically' (Jackson 2006) and those of Butt (2008) could provide a useful context to consider the purpose and relevance of GIS for future life and work, including how it may be used to bridge the divide between school geography and university geography, and between school geography and workplace geography.
- Given that motivation remains, de facto, a hugely important justification for using ICT in the classroom, a deeper investigation of *why* pupils enjoy using certain aspects of GIS (rather than simply acknowledging that they do) could be fruitful. Looking at motivation in relation to geographical learning outcomes, raising questions such as how GIS can support individual and situational interest and the perceived relevance of the subject by students could be valuable foci.

Further reading

1 Bednarz, S. (2001) *Thinking Spatially: Incorporating Geographic Information Science in Pre and Post Secondary Education*, think piece for Geographical Association, Sheffield: Geographical Association. Online, available at: www.geography.org.uk/download/EVbednarzthink.doc. This is a well-balanced paper, which clearly and critically presents the argument for using GIS in school teaching and learning.
2 Gersmehl, P.J. and Gersmehl, C.A. (2006) Wanted: a concise list of neurologically defensible and assessable spatial thinking skills. *Research in Geographic Education*, volume 8, pp. 5–38. This paper helps in understanding the concept of spatial thinking, and so to become clearer on how GIS might help students to think spatially.
3 O'Connor, P. (2007) Progressive GIS. *Teaching Geography*, Autumn 2007. Sheffield: Geographical Association, pp. 147–150. This article breaks down GIS skills and helps in understanding their progression.

References

Audet, R.H. (1993) *Developing a theoretical basis for introducing geographical information systems into high schools: cognitive implications.* Unpublished doctoral dissertation. Boston University, School of Education.

BECTA (2004) *What the Research Says About Using ICT in Secondary Geography.* London: BECTA.

Bednarz, S. (2001) *Thinking Spatially: Incorporating Geographic Information Science in Pre and Post Secondary Education.* Think piece for Geographical Association, Sheffield: Geographical Association. Online, available at: www.geography.org.uk/download/EVbednarzthink.doc.

Butt, G. (2008) Is the future secure for geography education? *Geography*, 93(3): 158–165.

Cassidy, A. (2005) *Cyberworlds and learning geography.* Unpublished essay in part fulfilment of MA Geography in Education, IOE, University of London.

Fargher, M.G. (2004) *An investigation into the effectiveness of using GIS to enhance spatial skills in enquiry-based learning.* Unpublished dissertation in part fulfilment of MA Geography in Education, IOE, University of London.

Fargher, M.G. (2008) *Critical and participatory GIS.* Unpublished paper for Geography Education Research seminar, 26 November, IOE, University of London.

Firth, R. and Biddulph, M. (2009) Whose life is it anyway? Young people's geographies, in Mitchell, D. (ed.) *Living Geography – Exciting Futures for Teachers and Students.* London: Chris Kington Publishing, pp. 13–27.

Gardner, H. (1983) *Frames of Mind: the Theory of Multiple Intelligences.* New York: Basic Books.

Gersmehl, P.J. and Gersmehl, C.A. (2006) Wanted: a concise list of neurologically defensible and assessable spatial thinking skills. *Research in Geographic Education*, volume 8, pp. 5–38.

Golledge, R.G. and Stimson, R.J. (1997) *Spatial Behavior: a Geographic Perspective.* New York: Guilford Press.

Hidi, S. and Ainley, M. (2002) Interest and adolescence, in Pajares, F. and Urdan, T. (eds) *Academic Motivation of Adolescents.* Charlotte: Information Age Publishing, pp. 247–276.

Holloway, S.L. and Valentine, G. (2000) *Children's Geographies: Playing, Living, Learning.* London: Routledge.

Jackson, P. (2006) Thinking geographically, *Geography*, 91(1): 199–204.

Kerski, J. (2003) The implementation and effectiveness of GIS technology and methods in secondary education. *Journal of Geography*, 102(3): 128–137.

Lambert, D. (2008) *Living Geography*. Unpublished paper to UK Geography Teacher Educators conference, Bristol, 31 January.

Lambert, D. and Morgan, J. (2009) *Geography 11–19, a Conceptual Approach*. Milton Keynes: Open University Press.

Lidstone, J. and Stoltman, J. (2006) Editorial: searching for, or creating, knowledge: the roles of Google and GIS in geographical education. *International Research in Geographical and Environmental Education*, 15(3): 205–209.

Martin, F. (2006) Using ICT to create better maps, in Balderstone, D. (ed.) *The Secondary Geography Handbook*. Sheffield: Geographical Association, pp. 106–122.

Massey, D. (2005) *For Space*. London: SAGE Publications.

Mitchell, D. (2009) GIS: changing life and work, in Mitchell, D. (ed.) *Living Geography*. London: Chris Kington Publishing, pp. 133–150.

Morgan, J. and Lambert, D. (2005) *Teaching School Subjects: Geography*. London: RoutledgeFalmer.

National Research Council (2006) *Learning to Think Spatially. Report of the Committee on Support for Thinking Spatially: the Incorporation of Geographic Information Science Across the K-12 Curriculum*. Washington, DC: The National Academies Press.

O'Connor, P. (2007) Progressive GIS. *Teaching Geography*, Autumn: 147–150.

Ofsted (2008) *Geography in Schools: Changing Practice*. London: Ofsted.

Roberts, M. (2003) *Learning Through Enquiry – Making Sense of Geography in the Key Stage 3 Classroom*. Sheffield: Geographical Association.

Robertson, M. and Fluck, A. (2004) Capacity building in geographical education: strategic use of online technologies. *Geography*, 89(3): 269–273.

Schuurman, N. (2000) Trouble in the heartland: GIS and its critics in the 1990s. *Progress in Human Geography*, 24(4): 569–590. Online, available at: www.sfu.ca/gis/schuurman/cv/PDF/2000PHG.pdf.

Schuurman, N. and Pratt, G. (2002) Care of the subject: feminism and critiques of GIS. *Gender, Place and Culture*, 9(3): 291–299. Online, available at: www.sfu.ca/gis/schuurman/cv/PDF/2003GPC.pdf.

Sieber, R.E. (2000) Conforming (to) the opposition: the social construction of geographical information systems in social movements. *International Journal of Geographical Information Science*, 14: 775–793.

Skelton, T. and Valentine, G. (1998) *Cool Places: Geographies of Youth Cultures*. London: Routledge.

Wiegand, P. (2006) *Learning and Teaching with Maps*. London: Routledge.

8 Assessment, teaching and learning

Paul Weeden

Recently, Assessment for Learning (AfL) has been promoted within schools through the Assessment for Learning Strategy (CIEA/DCSF/QCA 2008). Teachers have found this helpful because it provides a 'recipe book' of techniques that can readily be used within the classroom. However, without a real understanding of the underlying principles of Assessment for Learning, the Strategy may not produce the anticipated progress for individual learners. The focus of this chapter is to explore how the 'spirit' of Assessment for Learning can be used to help young people make progress in their learning and thereby improve their attainment in geography. This chapter highlights the importance of feedback and its complex nature.

A note about terminology. Although it is recognised that in formative assessment it is the feedback (and not the assessment itself) that is used formatively, in this chapter the term 'Assessment *for* learning' is used interchangeably with the term 'formative assessment', and 'Assessment *of* learning' is equated with 'summative assessment'.

The aims of this chapter are:

*   to understand how perceptions of Assessment for Learning may influence pedagogy.
*   to consider the purposes of assessment.
*   to explore the meaning of the term 'Assessment for Learning'.

Perceptions of assessment and learning

Assessment has long been recognised as important in education. Stobart has identified three characteristics of assessment that make it an important influence within schools and society.

*   Assessment is a value-laden social activity, and there is no such thing as 'culture-free' assessment.
*   Assessment does not objectively measure what is already there, but rather creates and shapes what is measured – it is capable of 'making up people'.

•   Assessment impacts directly on what and how we learn, and can under-
    mine or encourage effective learning.

                                                         (Stobart 2008: 1)

These ideas are challenging because they question commonly accepted
perceptions of assessment. The first of these assertions reminds us that curriculum and assessment are social constructions. In designing a geography curriculum or assessment, what gets included and what is left out? Who makes
these decisions? How are priorities decided and how have these changed over
time? For example, is the skill of being able to use GIS or an atlas now more
important than the capes and bays knowledge of the early twentieth century?
When assessments are designed, does the phrasing or structure of the question
influence the outcome? Why is it easier to assess knowledge and skills rather
than understanding or values and attitudes?

An example of the changing social construction of assessment comes from
the National Curriculum. When first designed in the early 1990s, the assessment structure consisted of lists of content to be assessed. The current formulation is in more generalised 'levels' that are broadly based on the
conceptualisation of progress in geography outlined in Box 8.1. In both cases
the criteria reflects different priorities of what is valuable in geography and
have been the subject of considerable debate.

Box 8.1 Aspects of progression in geography

•   Precision and sophistication in the vocabulary, language and grammar
    of geography.
•   Breadth and complexity of understanding at a range of scales.
•   Use of generalised knowledge, abstract ideas and linkage.
•   Maturity of understanding of issues, values and attitudes.
•   Independence in using the enquiry process and geographical skills (use
    of reasoning, explanations, linkages and judgements).

                        (Adapted from Bennetts and Rawling; quoted in
                                              Weeden and Butt 2009)

The assertion that assessment will 'make up' learners can be illustrated by
considering two common views of learners (after Dweck; quoted in Stobart
2008: 145):

•   Learners have a fixed amount of ability and our assessment is geared
    towards measuring competence.
•   Learning is related to effort, can be incremental and results in improving
    competence.

Stobart argues that the traditions of the English education system implicitly
tend towards the first view of learners, even if the language used by

policy-makers and schools suggests otherwise. Why is it that, despite all the efforts of government and teachers, children from deprived backgrounds are less likely to meet the expected standards? The early history of the development of assessment is one of trying to identify 'intelligence' or 'ability' and using this to place individuals in a known place within the education system. Examinations were created to make selection and certification fairer but class, racial, gender and socio-economic factors still influence an individual's success within the system. It is worth considering whether these factors are consciously acknowledged in schools (see Stobart 2008). When students are assessed and placed into sets early in their secondary-school career, what effect does this have upon their self-esteem and what impact does the 'label' have on teachers' perceptions of students?

This links to Stobart's third assertion that assessment can have a profound effect on the learning, motivation and self-esteem of students. Everyone can identify situations where an assessment has been a highly emotional or significant event that has affected their motivation and self-esteem. The way an individual will respond is complex and will depend on many different factors that vary with the context. This makes the teacher's role in giving feedback and raising student's self-esteem complex.

> Where the classroom culture focuses on rewards, 'gold stars', grades or place-in-the-class ranking, then students look for the ways to obtain the best marks rather than at the needs of their learning. The reported consequence is that where they have any choice, students tend to avoid difficult tasks. They also spend time and energy looking for the 'right answer'. Many are reluctant to ask questions out of fear of failure. Students who encounter difficulties and poor results are led to believe that they lack ability, and this belief leads them to attribute their difficulties to a defect in themselves about which they cannot do a great deal. So they 'retire hurt', avoid investing effort on learning which could only lead to disappointment, and try to build up their self-esteem in other ways. While high achievers can do well in such a culture, the overall result is to enhance the frequency and the extent of underachievement. What is needed is a culture of success, backed by a belief that all can achieve.
>
> (Black and Wiliam 1998a, b)

Purposes of assessment

There are many different purposes for assessments, but it is useful to classify them as:

*   selection and certification;
*   determining and raising standards;
*   formative assessment – Assessment *for* Learning (AfL).

(After Stobart 2008: 16)

There are overlaps between all three purposes, but the first purpose is most commonly associated with the outcome of a school career and agencies external to schools – the summative grades achieved in GCSE, A-levels or other qualifications, and the doors opened or closed as a result. The other two are more likely to be internal to schools and should be closely linked with teaching and learning. All three purposes have been the subject of a number of government initiatives in England over the last 20 years. Changes to external examinations have made them more closely controlled by government agencies, and the introduction of the National Curriculum in the early 1990s was intended to create a national system of assessment by which students' progress through their school careers could be more systematically and coherently monitored.

An assessment might be used for any of these three purposes. Approaches and outcomes will be different. It may be difficult, if not impossible, to satisfactorily achieve all three purposes at any one time, so it is important to sort out which purpose is prioritised in a particular teaching situation. This leads to the concept of 'fitness for purpose' or 'is the form of assessment appropriate for the intended outcome?' For example, if the intention is that learners are able to use GIS to analyse patterns of rainfall, would a test of their knowledge of weather symbols be appropriate?

Teachers and schools are therefore being encouraged to use two different but complementary assessment systems – one summative, the other formative. Most students, parents, teachers, schools and policy-makers see assessment largely in terms of the summative purpose – making judgements against national standards (e.g. National Curriculum Levels, GCSE, A-level grades). For many teachers, summative outcomes are prioritised because the performance of schools is largely judged by these results. This may encourage schools to focus on improving students' scores in tests ('teaching to the test') rather than focusing on improving learning.

This focus on summative outcomes may lead to confusion for teachers and schools about incorporating Assessment for Learning (AfL) into everyday teaching. AfL is the use of assessment strategies on a day-to-day basis as part of teaching to improve learning. AfL is not just collecting data about performance every few weeks to check whether students are reaching an expected target. The teacher or student must use the assessment information to inform future action – the next steps to be taken.

Assessing Pupils' Progress (APP) (QCA 2008a) is an attempt by QCA to rationalise the tensions between formative and summative assessment as part of their attempts to design and implement a coherent 11–19 curriculum (QCA 2008b). APP suggests that AfL is part of the day-to-day process of teaching and learning. Summative judgements are made less frequently (as periodic and transitional assessment) and should be less important than developing independent successful learners who can make judgements for themselves about the quality of their work.

Put the learner at the heart of assessment

Assessment should draw a picture of the whole individual and support the planning for their learning journey. It should develop motivated and successful independent learners who work confidently with others to evaluate the quality of their work, identify how it can be improved, and take action. Assessment should be much more than assigning a number or a letter – it is an essential tool to support learners and their learning.

(QCA 2008b)

APP therefore attempts to integrate formative assessment processes with summative data collection. It also implies a shift from the teacher making all the assessment judgements to one where there is a dialogue between student and teacher, and ultimately the student being able to make realistic judgements separately from the teacher. Day-to-day work should therefore be formative with the focus on the dialogue between student and teacher to develop understanding of how to improve and the next steps. However, this is undertaken within a framework where periodic and transitional judgements of overall performance are made that are summative and linked to national standards (such as the National Curriculum levels). The danger is that these summative judgements may exert an undue influence on day-to-day AfL activities.

It is therefore important to distinguish between formative and summative assessment. Both are important but teachers need to understand the differences and the contexts in which they are used (Box 8.2).

Box 8.2 The purposes associated with formative and summative assessment

*Formative assessment (Assessment **for** Learning)*

This usually involves relatively informal, day-to-day processes which inform both teacher and pupil about achievements. A key feature is the *feedback* for both teachers and students so that the future path of learning is (more) successful. Students should develop a better understanding of what is expected and how they can improve so that they can become more independent learners. Teachers should have a better understanding of how effective their teaching has been in promoting learning, and can *diagnose* particular difficulties that individual students face in the learning process. Students should be encouraged to identify for themselves the areas where they have problems. The key here is that performance is *ipsative* (compared against the student's previous work) and *personalised*.

*Summative assessment (Assessment **of** Learning)*

The purpose of this assessment is to measure achievement at the end of a unit of work, academic year or key stage. Ideally this measurement can be compared with judgement of other teachers nationally so teachers (and students/parents) need to know the *criteria* against which the judgement is made. Feedback tends to be limited to a mark, level or grade. There is usually little attempt to use the information to improve work but the data may be used to provide teachers and students/parents with information about the levels of achievement/attainment gained at different points on an educational course or programme. Sometimes the information will *certificate* achievement through the award of a certificate, or qualification (such as GCSE, GCE A-level or a vocational qualification), which has an accepted currency amongst students, teachers, parents and employers. Data collected from summative assessments can be used to *evaluate* the effectiveness of a school or department. Percentages of students who 'pass' qualifications at different levels (such as, say, the percentage of students in a school who gain 5 A*-to-C grades at GCSE) may be used as a way of evaluating the quality of teaching and learning.

(Adapted from Weeden and Butt 2009)

What is Assessment for Learning?

The process of seeking and interpreting evidence for use by learners and their teachers, to identify where the learners are in their learning, where they need to go to and how best to get there.

(Assessment Reform Group 2002: 2–3)

Unfortunately AfL is not well understood by many teachers.

I saw marking, testing and assessment as synonymous. Too often a mark out of ten and a comment, perhaps along the lines of 'Good', 'Good effort' or 'Poor' were all the students received when their books were returned. After an exam or test, the pupil generally received a percentage, class average and maybe a position in the class.

(McCleave 2002: 7)

This form of marking is summative because little was done with the data collected apart from entering it in a mark book or a school database, and the feedback provided did not help students know what to do next. The judging of schools and departments by their success in external examinations reinforces this idea that assessment is about judging performance through examinations and formal tests. Changing teachers' practice so assessment evidence is used formatively on a daily basis in their everyday teaching activities to help students become more independent learners has been more problematic.

A key text promoting AfL was *Inside the Black Box*, the summary of a systematic research review by Black and Wiliam (1998b). The research review used the evidence from studies where learning gains could be measured and came to the conclusion there were five 'key factors' in making Assessment for Learning integral to teaching and learning:

- The active involvement of students in their own learning.
- The provision of effective feedback to students.
- Adjusting teaching to take account of the results of assessment.
- The need for students to be able to assess themselves and understand how to improve.
- A recognition of the profound influence that assessment has on the motivation and self-esteem of students, both of which are crucial influences on learning.

(Assessment Reform Group 1999: 4)

These key factors have been translated into a number of classroom techniques that have been promoted and will be familiar to many teachers (see, for example, Clarke 2005; Weeden and Lambert 2006; Stobart 2008).

Clarity about learning intentions and success criteria. This involves the teacher being clear in their own mind on what they are hoping will be achieved and how success will be judged. Clarke (2005) suggests it is better to separate context and learning objectives so that students can see that the learning intention is generalisable and transferable to other contexts (see Table 8.1). However it is not enough for the teacher to be clear about learning intentions – they need also to be shared with the students.

Questioning. If teachers and students are to find out 'where they are in their learning', then the use of 'rich questions' are important. This contrasts with the questions commonly asked in most classrooms, which tend to be closed and factual. Strategies for rich questions include increasing the wait time (the time between a teacher asking a question and taking an answer) so that longer, more reasoned answers are given, more students answer, they are able to comment, expand on or give alternative explanations. Other strategies include jotting down ideas before answering, using whiteboards or 'no hands' so that everyone is expected to attempt an answer. The teacher's role is to act as a facilitator and encourage students to try to answer, and also for students to listen carefully to the answers from their peers. Sometimes questions can be used to encourage learners to reflect both on what they think and what they have heard from others (*What can we add to Javed's answer? Which parts of Suzie's answer would you agree with?*) This is an essential stage in shaping understanding, but teachers need to be patient and wait for the various ideas and thoughts to be revealed before they start correcting and curbing the direction of the discussion.

Table 8.1 Developing more generalisable learning intentions

Original learning intention	Revised learning intention	Context
To produce a questionnaire about shopping patterns.	To be able to investigate the distribution of an economic activity.	Interviews with people about where they shop and how their shopping patterns have changed.

Source: Clarke, S. 2005.

Feedback. This is the key strategy in students knowing their 'next steps' and aims to help students close the gap between current and intended perform-ance. However, increasingly it is recognised that providing feedback is a complex process and that feedback does not always promote learning. A number of factors that influence the effectiveness of feedback have been iden-tified. They include the:

• context in which it is provided,
• timing,
• focus.

  It is better to focus on the *task* by looking at the strengths and weaknesses of the work and encouraging all students to see what they can do better. If the feedback focuses on the *self* through the use of comments such as 'good work' or 'try harder' then it tends to be unhelpful because low attainers are discouraged and high attainers may avoid tasks if they think they won't perform well.

• use of praise and rewards,
• use of marks, grades or comments

  ... the understanding of formative assessment principles is difficult enough, let alone implementing those principles effectively into a class-room.... it would take a major shift to move most teachers away from the 'mark out of ten' system.

  (McCleave 2002: 7–8)

Black and Wiliam report that the research suggests encouraging students to engage with and act on comments will result in more progress than when marks or grades are used. This is because marks or grades give no indication of what to do next (see Stobart 2008, chapter 7, for a useful discussion of issues with providing effective feedback).

Self and peer assessment. This emphasises the active nature of the learning by the student and encourages them to take responsibility for judgements about the quality of their own and others' work. It requires the creation of a culture in the classroom where students are increasingly able to recognise good per-formance and where they are in their own learning. It encourages the use of metacognition (students thinking about their thinking and learning). The teacher's role is more facilitative, exploring their understanding of assessment with the students (*Which of these paragraphs is better? Why?*) and modelling how to provide effective feedback.

Dissertation summary

Andrew McCleave (2002) 'An Investigation into the Effective Implementation of Formative Assessment Principles in the Classroom'

This dissertation illustrates how one teacher's understanding of formative assessment has developed through his reading of the literature, and attempts to change his practice. The account illustrates how McCleave developed his understanding of the pedagogical ideas that underpin Assessment for Learning (formative assessment) and attempted to implement them within his teaching. Through the account there is a critique of previous practice, a developing understanding of the possibilities that AfL provides alongside an appraisal of the context in which change was attempted.

In his literature review, McCleave discusses how his reading of the literature has shifted his perspective of teacher assessment from marking books, correcting basic errors and the giving of marks (a 'bolt-on' activity) to one where it is more integral to both teaching and learning. The literature review considers different purposes of assessment and technical issues such as validity, reliability, manageability and fitness for purpose. There is discussion of the tension between formative and summative purposes of assessment and being 'trapped in a system which is dominated by notions of external accountability'. The relationship of assessment to both learning theories and motivation is considered. He concludes that change in classrooms is unlikely to occur soon while teachers are dominated by the current system.

He analysed the assessment policy and practices of the department, finding that the policy was focused almost entirely on the needs of the teacher rather than emphasising developing students' independent learning (the 'Trojan Horse'). It also highlighted the inconsistency in practice within the department and the lack of discussion between staff about 'standards' and expectations. 'Overall the policy concentrates too much on when and where, and not enough on how' (2002: 45).

The School assessment policy was also analysed, highlighting the confusion that teachers, students and parents had in understanding the systems in operation:

> At a recent parents' evening, concerns were raised by many by the lack of what they considered to be 'real' reporting. The progress reports with their pages of numbers and letters, were confusing and did not give a clear picture of their children's progress and current achievement.
>
> (2002: 46–47)

Reflection on his own practice identified limitations with regard to 'good practice' identified in the literature.

For his methodology McCleave considers different styles of research within geography education with a particular focus on action and case-study research. To make the study manageable, he focused on two AfL techniques (feedback and self-assessment) from the wide range in the literature. These were operationalised with two classes – from Year 8 and Year 11. Devising a criteria-referenced mark scheme for Year 8 required McCleave to engage with progression in geography in a new way, and he also worked with other members of the department to reach a common understanding of standards. One key feature was an attempt to remove comments that focused merely on neatness and presentation and instead to look at what made the work 'better geography'. Although the research focus was on teacher change, he attempted to 'measure the effect on students' (2002: 74) through the use of quantitative and qualitative data.

In analysing his results, McCleave comments on the small sample size and the difficulty of interpreting the data in meaningful ways. The use of questionnaires and interviews for different groups are justified, and there are comments about the success or otherwise of the strategies. In his conclusion McCleave evaluates the data-collection methods and the success of strategies used. The difficulties of coding are discussed. The implications of the research are highlighted and comments made about the difficulty of effecting change in the classroom.

McCleave's research demonstrates one teacher's tentative steps along the road to developing his understanding of AfL. He demonstrates how his thinking has altered and some of the barriers to successful implementation of change. The changes made are small-scale but there is evidence of successful outcomes.

For discussion

The key idea being developed here is that the use of Assessment for Learning techniques is more complex than the AfL strategy suggests. This is because:

- AfL techniques are being implemented within a context that prioritises the summative and accountability purposes;
- the apparently simple AfL techniques identified in the literature may require a substantial shift in teacher's conceptions of and approaches to pedagogy;
- AfL should meet both the current needs of students and help them to develop self-regulation skills that are transferable.

There are many possible starting points for further investigations because the literature provides a number of assertions about the effectiveness of AfL techniques in raising standards that can be investigated. Some of these have been indicated in the chapter, such as the use of comments rather than marks and grades, different forms of feedback, rich questions, self- and peer-assessment, clarifying and sharing learning intentions.

It should be remembered that making changes to assessment practice and implementing these techniques will take time and is likely to be most successful within a school context that is supportive and where teachers:

- understand the different purposes of assessment;
- understand how using AfL activities may change the teacher's role;
- espoused views of assessment match their practice.

Further reading

1 Black, P. and Wiliam, D. (1998a) 'Assessment and classroom learning', *Assessment in Education: Principles, Policy and Practice*, 5(1), pp. 7–73. The full research review outlining why AfL improves classroom learning.
2 Black, P. and Wiliam, D. (1998b) *Inside the Black Box*. London: NFER Nelson. The best-selling pamphlet that summarises the key findings of the research review in a easily digestible form.
3 Black, P., Harrison, C., Lee, C., Marshall, B. and Wiliam, D. (2003) *Assessment for Learning: Putting it into Practice*. Maidenhead: Open University Press. An account of the outcomes of the Kings, Medway, Oxford research project on the implementation of AfL in the classroom. Lots of suggestions about implementation of AfL and commentary on the barriers to change.
4 Clarke, S. (2005) *Formative Assessment in the Secondary Classroom*. London: Hodder and Stoughton. A practical guide to implementing effective AfL in the classroom.
5 Gardner, J. (ed.) (2006) *Assessment and Learning*. London: Sage. This volume provides a comprehensive view of assessment used to support learning by the members of the Assessment Reform Group.
6 Stobart, G. (2008) *Testing Times: the Uses and Abuses of Assessment*. London: Routledge. This text argues that assessment shapes how we see ourselves and how we learn. Challenges the labelling of learners by ability and provides a theoretical underpinning for AfL.
7 Weeden, P. and Lambert, D. (2006) *Geography Inside the Black Box*. London: NFER Nelson. Written specifically for geography teachers, this pamphlet summarises some of the key ways that AfL can be incorporated into the classroom.
8 Weeden, P. and Butt, G. (eds) (2009) *Assessing Progress in Your Key Stage 3 Geography Curriculum*. Sheffield: Geographical Association. A practical guide to assessing the new Key Stage 3 curriculum. Provides guidance on incorporating effective AfL into a school framework that requires regular reporting of assessment data.

References

Assessment Reform Group (1999) *Assessment for Learning: Beyond the Black Box*. Online, available from: www.qca.org.uk/libraryAssets/media/beyond_black_box2. pdf (accessed 18 January 2009).

Assessment Reform Group (2002) *Assessment for Learning 10 Principles: Research-based Principles to Guide Classroom Practice*. Online, available from: www.qca.org.uk/libraryAssets/media/4031_afl_principles.pdf (accessed 15 December 2008).

Black, P. and Wiliam, D. (1998a) 'Assessment and classroom learning'. *Assessment in Education: Principles, Policy and Practice*, 5(1): 7–73.

Black, P. and Wiliam, D. (1998b) *Inside the Black Box*. London: NFER Nelson.

CIEA/DCSF/QCA (2008) *The Assessment for Learning Strategy*. Online, available from: http://publications.teachernet.gov.uk/eOrderingDownload/DCSF-00341–2008.pdf (accessed 15 December 2008).

Clarke, S. (2005) *Formative Assessment in the Secondary Classroom*. London: Hodder and Stoughton.

Hargreaves, E. (2005) 'Assessment for learning? Thinking outside the (black) box'. *Cambridge Journal of Education*, 35(2): 213–224.

McCleave, A. (2002) *An Investigation into the Effective Implementation of Formative Assessment Principles in the Classroom*. London: Institute of Education, Unpublished Masters Dissertation

QCA (2008a) *Assessing Pupils' Progress: Assessment at the Heart Of Learning*. Online, available from: http://qca.org.uk/libraryAssets/media/12707_Assessing_Pupils_Progress_leaflet_-_web.pdf (accessed 15 December 2008).

QCA (2008b) *Designing and Implementing a Coherent 11–19 Curriculum*. London: QCA (ref: QCA/08/3863).

Stobart, G. (2008) *Testing Times: the Uses and Abuses of Assessment*. London: Routledge.

Weeden, P. and Lambert, D. (2006) *Geography Inside the Black Box*. London: NFER Nelson.

Weeden, P. and Butt, G. (eds) (2009) *Assessing Progress in Your Key Stage 3 Geography Curriculum*. Sheffield: Geographical Association.

9 Beyond a tokenistic multiculturalism

Hakhee Kim

Multiculturalism, post-colonialism and anti-racism remain relevant issues in geography education. The term 'inclusion' has also become a relevant issue, featuring strongly in many government documents and initiatives. Each government strategy and curriculum now makes explicit reference to how it can contribute to the inclusive agenda. The discipline of geography has a history of dealing with issues around inclusion and multiculturalism, and there is much that can be learnt from developments in academic geography in understanding inclusion that has practical implications for the geography classroom. This chapter does not seek to describe an inclusive classroom, as these debates are well-rehearsed elsewhere. Instead the chapter seeks to explore how geographical thinking can go beyond tokenistic inclusive or multicultural education. Practical strategies to free our thinking from the limits imposed by dualistic structures such as *First* and *Third* World or *rich North* and the *poor South* can be developed in education arenas. It is possible to disrupt these dichotomies by locating and contextualising knowledge and world views in their particular contexts. Furthermore, alternative narratives and educational themes can be used to tackle racism and colonialism. This chapter suggests that the concept of 'situated knowledge' can open new opportunities to challenge the stereotyping of developing countries and help us to move beyond a tokenistic approach to inclusion by acknowledging the validity of different perspectives and local knowledges.

The aims of this chapter are:

- to go beyond a 'boutique' multiculturalism through a critical, reflective and empathetic geography education that is sensitive to context.
- to reveal how critical pedagogy and geographical imaginations can shed light on hidden realities.
- to understand the multi-dimensionality of racial and multicultural issues.

Critical multicultural pedagogy

Multicultural discourse and practice are receiving considerable attention in the field of education (Bennett 2001). Discourses such as post-modernism, post-structuralism and post-colonialism offer alternative ways of rethinking binaries like self/other and here/there in multicultural education (Martin and van Gunten 2002). Asher (2007) proposes a critical multicultural pedagogy which unpacks the tensions of race, culture, gender and sexuality in dialogical and self-reflexive ways and criticises the conventional approaches in inclusive education. She insists that dominant ideas in Western cultural systems help to maintain the status quo by silencing and closeting difference.

Although multicultural and anti-racist approaches to British geography teaching in the 1980s were gaining strength, some of the progress was hindered with the introduction of the National Curriculum following the 1988 Education Reform Act (Morgan and Lambert 2003). The voices calling for education to reflect the multicultural diversity of British society have since gathered strength despite the considerable time and curriculum constraints that confront teachers.

Critical education theorists such as Michael Apple and Henry Giroux provide a meta-analysis of the function of schools in capitalistic societies and the effects of its pedagogies on students from diverse background. They argue that to transform the nature of teaching and learning requires work at multiple levels and the development of situated understandings of teaching and learning in classrooms and the larger social context (McLaren 2006: 177). A critical inclusive education would encourage students to engage with diverse ideas and go beyond the boundaries of Western thinking and viewpoints to engage with ideas from elsewhere. The central point of critical education involves helping people to confront the ways that understanding knowledge has changed and to contextualise all teaching and learning. Critical education envisions a consciously examined, critical and deliberately constructed base rather than teaching in a knowledge-transmission, 'correct-answer-oriented' curriculum. These critical curricular and epistemological perspectives have a power to change the purpose of education.

Stanley Fish (1997) distinguishes between 'boutique multiculturalism' and 'strong multiculturalism'. He argues that boutique multiculturalism is characterised by its superficial relationships to the facets of other cultures (such as ethnic restaurants, weekend festivals etc.). He insists: 'A boutique multiculturalist may find something of value in rap music and patronize soul-food restaurants, but he will be uneasy about affirmative action and downright hostile to an afro-centrist curriculum' (Fish 1997: 378).

He argues that a boutique multiculturalist does not, and cannot, take seriously the core value of the other cultures. So the boutique multiculturalist cannot take seriously the core value of cultures other than their own, particularly when these conflict with a value of their own culture. Conversely, strong multiculturalism fosters the distinctiveness of all cultures and cultural traditions. A strong multicultralist will want to accord a deep respect to all cultures at their core, for they believe that each person has a right to form and nourish their own identity.

To accomplish a 'strong' and 'authentic' inclusive education, teachers should help students to seek the origins of the knowledge they teach and to ask questions concerning who benefits from particular descriptions of reality and landscapes. Such a critical and analytical ability would alert students to the power politics involved within resources such as textbooks. Teachers and students need to understand that knowledge is not only created in the researcher's laboratory or the academic's office, but in the consciousness produced during thinking, discussion, teaching, writing and conversation.

In the multicultural-education arena, this creation of knowledge takes on even more significance. When a teacher does not share the culture, language, race or socio-economic backgrounds of their students, she or he can become an explorer who works with students to create mutually understood texts. Based on their explorations, teachers and students create new learning materials full of mutually generated meanings and shared interpretations (McLaren 2006: 147). This is the inverse approach to the model of teacher as expert.

Situatedness of knowledge

So far, this chapter has explored these ideas within the context of the classroom. However, The situatedness of knowledge is also explored in debates in academic geography.

Gillian Rose (1993), a feminist geographer, suggests that the dominant way of looking in geography has been normalised as white, male and heterosexual. According to Rose (1993), conventionally, the Western academy has constructed the most valuable form of knowledge and refused to situate claims relative to personal, social and geographical contexts. However, 'situated knowledge' is the idea that all knowledge-claims – even scientific ones – are partial and located from within a particular perspective (Haraway 1991). Objectivity emerges through elaborating and understanding this partiality. This opens opportunities to acknowledge the validity of other perspectives and knowledges. The next section explores an example of how this process can help us to understand complex and controversial issues.

Resisting stereotypes

Prejudice is an attitude based on preconceived ideas of a subject and judgements about beliefs that are based on unsubstantiated or faulty information (Patel and Crocco 2003). Prejudices and stereotypes are learned from parents, peers, experiences in school, and societal messages in films, television and the news media. In the USA and other Western countries, combating stereotypes and prejudices at schools is one of major research genres and educational goals in multicultural education (Bennett 2001). Morgan and Lambert say: 'In geography education, multiculturalism involved a rewriting of the school curriculum and its texts so that they recognised the "ways of life" of people of "other culture" and avoided in the reproduction of crude stereotypes' (2003: 7).

Although multicultural education discourse is well-established theoretically, stereotypical representations of other cultures seem to persist in texts and school practices (Kim 2005; Smith 1999). This tendency persists with particular force in relation to Arab and Muslim peoples. Patel and Crocco (2003) showed that South Asians and Muslims are stereotyped in classrooms and Asher (2007: 65) finds in her teacher-training classes that students describe 'Middle-Eastern' women as monolithically oppressed and view Muslim culture as being essentially less advanced than Western culture.

For some, the Arab and Muslim world is dominated by images of the barren desert, the golden Mosque, Arabian Nights, veiled women. After the New York (9/11) and London (7/7) bombings, the Western public and media focused on Muslims, linking Muslims at large with terrorism (Ayish 2006; Modood and Ahmad 2007). Such superficial and stereotypical knowledges can re-enforce distorted understandings of the complex reality of the Arab and Muslim cultures.

Ahmad (2006) reveals a profound belief among British Muslims that the negative stereotyping, derogatory use of language and sensationalism of the major Western media after the events of 11 September 2001 contributed significantly to the increase in anti-Muslim attacks. News networks such as CNN, Sky News and the BBC were perceived to offer Eurocentric or US-biased news, and failed to depict the reality of Muslim worlds in their socio-political analysis. However, there seems to be little effort to include Arabs and diverse Muslims with other ethnic, racial and sexual-preference minorities in terms of corrective educational efforts.

Critical multicultural education can lead students to consider world poverty, global conflicts, social injustice and deprivation in the bigger picture of global power politics. Geography teachers can help students to frame news reports on Arabs and Muslims in the broader context with the global sense of geography. Through using teaching strategies that explore the diversity of the Muslim world and the real-life contexts of individual Muslims, students can rethink their own stereotypes about the Arab region and Muslims. The goal is to move away from a 'boutique' multiculturalism to an understanding of the complexity of other cultures with different values.

The issue of the *hijab* – also called a 'veil' or 'headscarf' – for Muslim women is an example that can be used to explore multiculturalism. Veiling, the covering of women's hair and sometimes their face and body, has figured prominently within Western representations of the Arab and Muslim world. Many Westerners believe *hijab* functions to oppress women (Gereluk 2005). The veiled woman symbolises the oppression of women in Arab and Muslim cultures and provides proof that these cultures need to be modernised and corrected.

However some Muslim women in the Western and Muslim world inscribe *hijab* with alternative meanings, such as defining Muslim identity, resisting sexual objectification, affording more respect, preserving intimate relationships, and even providing freedom (Droogsma 2007). A paradoxical situation occurs in a country such as Tunisia, where, although veiling has been banned in schools, universities and public administrations since 1990, it has assumed a different meaning within the life of some Tunisian Muslims. Some unveiled Muslim university students in Tunis argued that they wanted to wear veils in universities and public spaces – or, more accurately, have a choice to wear – to get more respect from their communities, show their devotion to God and avoid sexual objectification (Personal interview 2008).

More fundamental questions can be raised in the global context. Do Western women enjoy more freedom through being able to wear anything? In Western society, masculine cultural norms often dictate what is seen as being acceptable fashion for women, such as appropriate hair and make-up, tight clothing and high heels, which confines women physically and psychologically. Some 88 per cent of all cosmetic procedures were performed on women (Seager 2003). Women undergo a massive amount of suffering in the pursuit of beauty. Around the world, but especially in the developed countries, many women each year get painful and dangerous plastic surgery to conform to prevailing standards of beauty. An obsession with weight and body image has become an intrinsic part of the lives of women and girls in the capitalist world, and many suffer from eating disorders (Brumberg 2000; Colls 2006). Globalisation is accelerating the adoption of a monolithic Western beauty standard around the world through commercial advertisements, diverse media and things such as international beauty contests. There are now only few places in the world – mostly in Arab and Muslim countries – untouched by this commercial empire of beauty.

The meaning of veiling as 'dress' can be understood as broadly situated and individually practised (Gereluk 2005; Liederman 2000). Geography teachers can situate Muslim women's choices within broader contexts. To understand veiling as situated, embodied practice, it is necessary to view space as relational, something more than concerning an individual body. Space, whether sacred or profane, is not produced in a vacuum, but rather through a web of power relations that are themselves forged in a multiple scale from the local, the national and to the global. When it comes to Muslim women's issues, the diversity in a group's internal identity and the imposition of external simplistic stereotypes can be explored through geographical education.

New geographical imaginations

The above example has been used to illustrate one way that situated understandings can be illuminative. The general principle can be applied to much geographical content. Dividing the world into several regions may be a convenient and essential starting point for learning about the world (Lewis and Wigen 1997). However, prejudicial or stereotypical images of developing countries can prevent teachers and students from going beyond a 'boutique' multiculturalism. By taking simplistic approaches to the world economic system and development discourse based on the problematic geographical imagination, teachers can be caught in a vicious circle of encouraging a tokenistic multiculturalism. Even critical theorists trying to imagine an anti-racist and post-development era can hardly avoid repeating the rhetoric based on the conventional stereotypes of the Third World. The problem is that these stereotypes do an injustice to the complexities of the real world, which can lead to misconceptions and inaccurate geographical understanding (Kim 2007).

'Development', when applied to different countries, was often understood in terms of 'modernisation'. Escobar (1995) traces the discursive creation of the Third World as both the needy object of international-development intervention and the excuse for expansion of a new world power's mode of global governmentality. He considers why the Western mind-set defined the Third World as a miserable world of poverty, disease and backwardness that had to be mended by Western capital and technology. He examines how Western texts characterise the Third World as one homogenous place without any historical consideration.

Robinson (2003) argues that this contextualisation extends to how different countries are perceived as having and using knowledge. For example, local communities in the Third World can be stigmatised as backward, outside, behind and beneath the transcending fast lanes of modernisation and globalisation. Geographers are well equipped to understand this complexity. Development is diverse, complex and often contradictory, and the real-life experiences of people and the diversity of the minute local contexts should not be ignored or denigrated. Unpacking the concept of 'development' involves new perspectives on the development process and listening to other voices from the South. A revival of regional geography and its application to multicultural education could be also an extremely important step towards producing a postcolonial sensitivity in classrooms.

Critical analysis of these geographical frameworks can reveal how important it is to deconstruct how we categorise and teach about different places and people. Rethinking development means re-examining the categories used in development texts and revealing the historical, political, cultural and institutional relations that shape them (Broadberry and Gupta 2006; Frank 1998). We can map out a more complex geography that avoids dividing the world into simple binaries like rich/poor or North/South. Indeed, even politically correct terms like 'over-developed' or 'environmentally/socially poor' can be seen as too simplistic. The emphasis on the trans-national connectedness of regions and places is a possible way to avoid such stereotyping (Robinson 2003: 279). The politics of space as a social construction can be addressed from the micro-personal to the global scale. In the classroom, such a perspective can explore a range of geographical imaginations to categorise the world. Teaching with these geographical imaginations could be a meaningful step to grasp the complexities and interconnections of the real world without losing the global sense of geography. This is an exciting and innovative way of viewing inclusive education.

Dissertation summary

Emma Wellsted (2003) 'Learning About the Developing World: How Pupils Make Sense of Information Presented to Them'

Wellsted's dissertation focuses on how to challenge pupils' often partial, limited or negative views on developing countries by presenting diverse perspectives, through the careful choices of resources. It investigates how pupils make sense of information presented to them by examining the outcomes of a teaching unit on Malawi. Her premise is that if pupils can recognise that places have 'multiple identities' they may be likely to question media perspectives and bias.

The developing world is often perceived as a place which is reliant on Western aid for development, where the people are seen as victims, where extreme poverty and famine prevails, and where war, fear and oppression are the norm. Her first-hand experiences of travelling in Africa and teaching in Malawi are useful for building up a multi-dimensional picture of life there. She is passionate about giving pupils a 'gut' feeling about a place and sharing her experiences with her pupils. Her research shows that pupils are capable of moving from existing prejudices and misconceptions about the developing world to a more balanced and thoughtful view.

Her research questions are as follows:

- What sense do pupils make of information presented to them about places?
- How do pupils' views change as they learn about Malawi and to what extent can they recognise that their perceptions have changed?
- Which learning resources or lessons did pupils think helped to develop their understanding of what it is like to live in Malawi?
- What implications does this have for teaching about places?

The research was inspired by critical pedagogy and post-colonial geography. She used an action research methodology to analyse the level of understanding developed by one class of Year 8 pupils. An action research methodology encourages changes to take place as the researcher embarks upon a continual quest for better ways to teach. Her chosen methods to collect data were pupil diaries, an end-of-unit questionnaire and group interviews. They were later analysed to gain an in-depth understanding of the way pupils engage with the content and the extent to which they are able to evaluate their own learning. It is clear that pupils wanted access to 'authentic' material and to listen to the voices directly from the South.

In her literature review, she places issues on the developing world into context and critically reflects on the concept of development and the vocabulary that is used to describe the world's poorest countries. They can be classified as 'poor', 'underdeveloped', 'developing', 'Third World' or 'Global South', in spite of the obvious huge diversity between countries, each with their own distinct culture, political and economic differences. Such classifications are often used as a kind of 'verbal shorthand' as a way of simplifying reality, but they can also convey imperialistic ideology, with many descriptive terms that are at best inaccurate, and at worst pejorative. Focusing on Africa illustrates some powerful stereotypes that exist; for example, that it is a homogenous continent where people are starving, living in huts and where life is primitive. Wellsted points out that Europe's image of Africa has been 'hunger, skeletal children, dry and cracked earth, urban slums, massacres, AIDS and miserable refuges'. She insists that stereotypes discount the strengths and positive qualities of African people and create the impression that Britain has nothing to learn from them.

She adopted a model of valuing children's personal geographies as a starting point for geography education. It consists of three steps, such as 'Pre View', 'New View', and 'Re View':

- Identifying 'Pre View': recording what they already know.
- Developing their 'New View': working with a range of new source of information.
- Undertaking a 'Re View': explicitly comparing their 'Pre View' with their New View.

Pupils wrote a diary to show how they made sense of information and changed their perspective as they progressed through the unit, learning about different aspects of Malawian life. The pupils were introduced to a variety of resources which show different perspectives and 'multiple identities'. She encouraged pupils to adopt an enquiry approach by looking carefully at the visual materials, making connections between what is visible and what they already know, and to speculate and hypothesise.

Wellsted integrated her own life experiences and enthusiasm with her geography teaching. The unit aimed to take pupils on a 'virtual journey' to Malawi, by introducing her personal experiences and local voices to present students an authentic picture and a more balanced view on Malawi, including both positive and negative aspects. The unit incorporated topics that pupils could easily empathise with.

For discussion

- Can you find stereotypical images or descriptions of other cultures in your school geography textbooks, films, television and the news media?
- How do you use your or students' personal experiences and situated knowledges to stimulate students' interests in other countries and go beyond a tokenistic multiculturalism in geography classrooms?
- What kind of resources or tools do you adopt to include diverse worldviews and provide more balanced perspectives on development?

Further reading

1 Fish, S. (1997) Boutique multiculturalism, or why liberals are incapable of thinking about hate speech. *Critical Inquiry* 23(2): 378–395. For more on boutique multiculturalism.
2 Morgan, J. and Lambert, D. (2003) *Place, 'Race' and Teaching Geography*. Sheffield: Geographical Association. To explore these issues further.
3 Patel, V. and Crocco, M.S. (2003) Teaching about South Asian Women: getting beyond the stereotypes. *Social Education* 67(1): 22–26. For more on some of the issues raised in this chapter.

References

Ahmad, F. (2006) British Muslim perceptions and opinions on news coverage of September 11. *Journal of Ethnic and Migration Studies* 32(6): 961–982.

Asher, N. (2007) Made in the (multicultural) U.S.A.: unpacking tensions of race, culture, gender, and sexuality in education. *Educational Researcher* 36(2): 65–73.

Ayish, N. (2006) Stereotypes, popular culture, and school curriculum: how Arab American Muslim high school students perceive and cope with being the 'other', in Zabel, D.A. (ed.) *Arabs in the America: Interdisciplinary Essays on the Arab Diaspora*. New York: Peter Lang, 79–116.

Bennett, C. (2001) Genres of research in multicultural education. *Review of Educational Research* 71(2): 171–217.

Broadberry, S. and Gupta, B. (2006). The early modern great divergence: wages, prices and economic development in Europe and Asia, 1500–1800. *Economic History Review* LIX(1): 2–31.

Brumberg, J.J. (2000) *Fasting Girls: the History of Anorexia Nervosa*. New York: Vintage Books.

Colls, R. (2006) Outsize/outside: bodily bigness and the emotional experiences of British women shopping for clothes. *Gender, Place & Culture* 13(5): 529–545.

Droogsma, R.A. (2007) Redefining *Hijab*: American Muslim women's standpoints on veiling. *Journal of Applied Communication Research* 35(3): 294–319.

Escobar, A. (1995) *Encountering Development: the Making and Unmaking of the Third World*. Princeton: Princeton University Press.

Fish, S. (1997) Boutique multiculturalism, or why liberals are incapable of thinking about hate speech, *Critical Inquiry* 23(2): 378–395.

Frank, A.G. (1998) *Reorient: Global Economy in the Asian Age*. Berkeley: University of California Press.

Gereluk, D. (2005) Should Muslim headscarves be banned in French schools? *Theory and research in Education* 3(3): 259–271.

Haraway, D.J. (1991) *Simians, Cyborgs and Women: the Reinvention of Nature*. London: Free Association Books.

Kim, H. (2005) *Resisting the Stereotyped Southeast Asia Through Everyday Food*. Seoul National University Doctorial Thesis.

Kim, H. (2007) Does Geography 'really' contribute to ESD? Critical reflections on meta-geographical frameworks in World Geography. *Geographiedidaktische Forschungen* 42: 66–72.

Lewis, M.W. and Wigen, K. (1997) *The Myth of Continents*. Berkeley: University of California Press.

Liederman, L.M. (2000) Religious diversity in schools: the Muslim headscarf controversy and beyond. *Social Compass* 47(3): 367–381.

McLaren, P. (ed.) (2006) *Rage and Hope*. New York: Peter Lang Publishing.

Martin, R. and Van Gunten, D.M. (2002) Reflected identities: applying positionality and multicultural social reconstructionism in teacher education. *Journal of Teacher Education* 53(1): 44–54.

Modood, T. and Ahmad, F. (2007) British Muslim perspectives on multiculturalism. *Theory, Culture & Society* 24(2): 187–213.

Morgan, J. and Lambert, D. (2003) *Place, 'Race' and Teaching Geography*. Sheffield: Geographical Association.

Patel, V. and Crocco, M.S. (2003) Teaching about South Asian Women: getting beyond the stereotypes. *Social Education* 67(1): 22–26.

Robinson, J. (2003) Postcolonialising geography: tactics and pitfalls. *Singapore Journal of Tropical Geography* 24(3): 273–289.

Rose, G. (1993) *Feminism and Geography: the Limits to Geographical Knowledge*. Cambridge: Polity Press.

Seager, J. (2003) *The State of Women in the World Atlas* (3rd edition). London: Women's Press.

Smith, M.W. (1999) Teaching the 'Third World': unsettling discourses of difference in the school curriculum. *Oxford Review of Education* 25(4): 485–499.

10 Approaches to learning outside the classroom

Bob Digby

In 2006, the UK government published a manifesto for Learning Outside the Classroom (DfES 2006). It is an enthusiastic document, promoting many advantages and benefits for students for work done outside the classroom. It is liberal in its definition of 'outside', including anything from work done in the school grounds to formal trips and visits that may last minutes or weeks. It adds to a range of actions and policies that together form part of a family of initiatives known as 'Every Child Matters', whereby the Government's intent is for every child, irrespective of background or circumstances, to be given the support they need to be healthy, stay safe, to enjoy and achieve, to make a positive contribution, and to achieve economic well-being. Learning outside is seen as integral to this.

Learning outside the classroom is hardly new to geographers in schools. Fieldwork in the subject has a rich history, from the days of the school excursion and visits to classic locations in the early days of compulsory education, through to its status as a compulsory requirement in every GCSE specification since 1986 and most post-16 specifications in Curriculum 2000. However, the kind of fieldwork being experienced by students varies widely, created as it is by teachers and examination boards whose paradigms and pedagogies may give very different messages. Now that coursework is no longer present in post-16 specifications, the kinds of fieldwork that many students experience could change; certainly, there is a rich seam of experience to be researched about changing fieldwork across the curriculum in the post-2008 curriculum changes.

The aims of this chapter are:

- to explore the shifting paradigms and pedagogies and their influence upon geographical fieldwork.
- to explore the potential impacts of Learning Outside the Classroom, and how well placed geographers are to face up to these.
- to consider research opportunities that exist to investigate how and why fieldwork varies.

Shifting paradigms of geography and their influence

Systematic and regional geography – pre-1960

> *Regional Geography*: An approach to geography concerned with the study of regions and their areal differentiation.
>
> (Butt 2000: 157)

School geography was concerned with comprehensive coverage of the world. Textbooks were systematic accounts of physical and human geography, emphasising description and explanation; many were regional, covering continents in a factual manner with maps, photographs and text. Latterly, textbooks included 'sample studies' aimed at making geography more real.

Field trips were often, though not exclusively, residential for older groups of students, to see examples of places that they had studied. Teaching was usually didactic; a teacher would tell students what was happening at 'classic' locations, such as Malham. Students would take notes; their input was through labelled field sketching and annotated photographs. The outcome was usually an explanatory set of notes, illustrated with sketches and photos. The emphasis was mostly of a kind of teaching that Barnes (1976) describes as 'transmissive' (see Box 10.1), with the teacher as 'expert' and students as passive recipients of valued knowledge.

However, Job (1996) evaluates this kind of 'school excursion' more positively than others. 'Guided through the landscape by a skilled practitioner', he claims, students would gain a holistic view of a landscape, with its links to underlying geology clearly determined, and the human response as a synthesis of land use, soil types, local climate and slope. He cites Goudie (1994) in recognising the value of such an approach in support of maintaining a landscape tradition. Pedagogically, students may have been passive recipients of some handed-down creed; as a learning approach, it was uncritical and did little to further student understanding of contemporary people–environment issues. But the ability to see a landscape in this way helps students to 'interpret a landscape in its wholeness and thereby to grasp something of the essence of place' (Job 1996: 35).

Box 10.1 Pedagogy and fieldwork – the work of Douglas Barnes

Barnes (1976) saw teaching and learning as different processes, and that each is linked closely to the philosophies, outlooks and preferences of the teachers concerned. He based his ideas on hundreds of classroom observations, from which he characterised two kinds of teacher:

- The teacher who values knowledge and perceives it as their role to teach it to their students. He referred to this kind of teacher as 'transmissive', because of the way that they saw their role – i.e. to transmit knowledge. They were 'experts' and sought to develop that same expertise in others.

• The 'interpretative' teacher was someone for whom knowledge was prob-lematic, and who understood that, for any problem, there were different interpretations based upon people's values and preferences. Students might accept some proposals and reject others. Such classrooms would debate issues, and students would understand that all learning and phenomena have a context. Barnes was influenced by Bruner (1966); for him, the cur-riculum could only emerge as a framework of ideas.

The tables below summarise the contrasts between these two types in as far as they apply to fieldwork and work done outside the classroom. Although it is possible that teachers may have traits from both columns, Barnes found that these characteristics varied little; transmissive teachers were such most of the time, and interpretative teachers also varied little. Each was influenced by their philosophies about teaching and learning, and the relative roles of teachers and learners in the classroom. Barnes emphasised that there was no 'right' way, though it is hard to read his work without thinking that transmission is perhaps 'wrong' and interpretation 'right'.

Table 10.1 Teacher characteristics

The transmission teacher	*The interpretation teacher*
• The teacher is expert in their subject. • Expects to impart knowledge to students. • Teacher talk is a means by which s/he imparts information, or asks questions to check what students know. • Regards knowledge as an aim. • Students are 'vessels' to be filled with knowledge. • Asks students questions to which s/he already knows the answer. • Teacher talk dominates. • Classroom dialogue is almost always teacher–pupil–teacher. • Decides who shall speak, when they shall speak and the value of what is spoken.	• The teacher is a facilitator of learning, understanding their subject but seeing learning as having limitless possibilities. • Knowledge is a construct; it has different forms and people construct it differently. • Regards talk as an important process of learning; ideas are discussed, clarified, and opinions changed/challenged • Regards knowledge as an outcome. • Students are an essential resource in learning. • Asks students open questions that are problematic, with many or no answers. • Sets activities where students are encouraged to talk. In fieldwork, students research data and discuss them. • Operates a variety of dialogues – many of which may be pupil–pupil–pupil. • Manages who speaks by using ground rules for discussion; students give feedback from fieldwork and are valued.

Table 10.2 Fieldwork characteristics

Transmission fieldwork	Interpretative fieldwork
• Knowledge is recorded through notes. • Fieldwork and its outcomes are much the same each year, irrespective of student. • The teacher decides data-collection methods. • Information is important; understanding is the result of knowing more. Knowledge is therefore a starting point. • Fieldwork notes are a 'product'. • Writing-up fieldwork is done to record material for learning. • Note-making is directed, often from teacher material. • Fieldwork aims to give 'correct' material. • There are few variations in the expected conclusions that students give. 'Right' and 'wrong' are essential vocabulary. • Positive feedback is given on the basis of correct answers – as though students are to be congratulated for knowing something.	• Data are recorded which may vary considerably. • Fieldwork and its outcomes may vary from one year to another, because students and their methods differ. • Students may decide some or all data-collection methods. • Understanding is given as much space as information. Knowledge and understanding arrive out of findings. • Fieldwork findings are part of a cognitive process; they may be incomplete, and returned to later. • Writing is done in drafts and amended as understanding or evidence alters. • Activities involve students, with few notes. Fieldwork methods vary to suit the student. • Fieldwork aims to develop students' interpretation and analysis of data. • Things do not have to be 'right'; indeed, there may be no 'right'. Validity is accepted on the basis of evidence. • Rewards and positive feedback in class lessons are likely to be on the basis of contributions to discussions, effort in analysing or in re-drafting.

(Source: summary based on Digby 2008)

The 'quantitative revolution': 1960s–1970s

The so-called quantitative revolution sought to replace the traditional description of regional geography with an explanatory process-oriented science based on the testing of theories and the construction of laws

(Unwin 1992: 106)

School geography was, and remains, deeply influenced by the 'new' geography of the 1970s. Fed by a cohort of 'baby-boomers' trained to teach an increasing school population during the 1970s, it was promoted by a generation exposed to the ideas of the likes of Chorley and Haggett, and influenced by geographical texts from the USA which challenged the traditional descriptive approaches to systematic and regional geography; these generated data which threw out

Davisian notions of landscape cycles of evolution. Youthful streams were discarded as concepts in favour of fluvial dynamics which revealed the complexity of factors underlying stream development and river landforms. In schools, the new generation of teachers introduced both quantitative techniques and a particular way of looking at the world: a positivist, scientific approach based on the collection of data, hypothesis testing and a search for generalisations about spatial pattern and process. Geography became a *spatial science*. Physical geography was heavily influenced by systems theory and plate tectonics. Textbooks and exam syllabuses were influenced by the approach, including theoretical models, analysis and a scientific enquiry approach, using techniques such as correlation and chi-square. By 1980 few textbooks were still using a regional framework.

Field trips in consequence developed into an era of Wellington boots, stream flow meters, sediment measurement, etc., as a generation of students collected volumes of data to create their own input into the subject. The key was a 'search for order'; to generate data from a range of physical and human environments, whose findings would be constrained by the methods used and conditions, and which would establish greater conceptual understanding. Students might have different results, and interpret data differently, but here were the beginnings of serious student analysis, and skill development through, for example, graphs, charts. Human geography similarly used CBD land use, pedestrian counts and height of building surveys to adopt a social scientific approach. Job (1996: 35) describes how students 'felt a degree of ownership of the field study, having had some input' into its outcomes.

However, Job also criticises much of what happened then and of what remains. His arguments are detailed, but hinge upon these points:

- Many of the hypotheses were based on a priori models, which were, or have been since proved to be, invalid.
- These ideas were often reductionist and narrow, and too focused upon either human or physical geography, with little exploration of the relationships between them.
- In seeking generally applicable explanations of process, the uniqueness of places was overlooked; a complete contrast to what had gone before.
- There was little critical appraisal of what was studied; rivers were studied in terms of their own dynamics but without consideration of the human influences which might have affected them, for instance. Data were often viewed for their own ends in testing a hypothesis, without any further exploration of wider contexts or explanations.

Humanistic geography – 1970s onwards

Humanistic geography: concerned with the social construction and experience of place, space and landscape rather than the spatial confinement of peoples and societies.

(Johnston *et al.* 2000: 361)

School geography has had some considerable influence from humanistic geography. From the 1980s onwards, increasing attention was given to values, attitudes, beliefs and perceptions. While these broadened the dimensions of geographical enquiry, different viewpoints were often presented in textbooks as 'objective' evidence to be accepted rather then different ways of perceiving and understanding the world.

Field trips were greatly influenced – nay, revolutionised – by the development of the 16–19 Geography Project in the late 1970s and its widespread adoption by schools and colleges in the 1980s. The '16–19 approach' (Naish *et al.* 1987: 39) emphasised values as a core part of geographical enquiry, and introduced a wide degree of student autonomy in enquiry-based learning. Its geographical techniques included perception and bi-polar surveys, quantifying personal opinion and difference. This verified and balanced quantitative geography in the eyes of those school geographers who felt that physical geography was too greatly emphasised during the positivist revolution. The emergence of coursework at both 14–16 and 16–19 led to a creativity in range of topics investigated, particularly those that were issues-based, and to which there were strong political dimensions. Students adopted a very large degree of independence in the topics they studied, proposing an individual title, designing their own data-collection procedures, and presenting, interpreting, analysing and evaluating with a more reduced teacher input than had perhaps ever been seen before in the British subject-based educational system.

There is no doubt about the core influence of those who made up the 16–19 geography team at the Institute of Education in London; few can have influenced the post-16 geography curriculum as greatly in the UK at any time, until it became intrinsically entwined with politics and the government exerted greater control. Job (1996) identifies the strengths of the approach – the student autonomy, the focus upon asking questions, and the focus upon human mistreatment of the earth. But he takes issue with its highly localised – again, reductionist – perspectives that leave aside some of the bigger questions. He cites, for instance, whether investigations that explore whether a superstore should be built at X will ever look critically at the underlying nature of consumerism.

Radical geography in the 1980s and since

Radical Geography: a term introduced in the 1970s to describe the increasing volume of geographical writing critical of spatial science and positivism.... The critique began with the contemporary concerns of society, but later coalesced around a belief in the power of Marxian analysis.... It promoted a concern for the study of topics such as poverty, hunger, health and crime.

(Johnston *et al.* 2000: 670)

School geography was considerably influenced by 'radical geography'. Instead of simply focusing on themes, some books started to focus on issues and concerns such as quality of life, inequality, poverty both within and outside the UK, thereby earning the reputation as a 'geography of social concern'. In physical geography there was more emphasis on the environment and human impact on physical processes and the environment; landform and process management became a significant part of physical geography courses and exam syllabuses. Politically, this approach gained both supporters and opponents during the era of Thatcherism, often splintering the geography teaching community.

Field trips saw an expansion in enquiries that researched 'difference', for instance in measuring and adding value to notions of inequality. The surge in market-led 'Docklands-style' regeneration created investment poles and, by contrast, left other communities relatively deprived. Geographers in school sought to measure and record spatial deprivation with students. Fieldwork often involved teams of students investigating deprivation over a wide area, each team contributing data to a whole-group study. GCSE and post-16 coursework embedded this approach firmly, greatly influencing topics studied and engendering creativity in data collection. On the other hand, a greater degree of prescription by examination boards, together with advice from examiners in raising achievement, led to a degree of uniformity in designing and writing up fieldwork.

Postmodern: 1990s/present

> *Postmodernism*: a theoretical approach to human geography, which rejects the claims of grand theories and metanarratives. Instead it recognizes that all knowledge is partial, fluid and contingent and emphasises a sensitivity to difference and an openness to a range of voices.
>
> (Valentine 2001: 345)

> postmodernists insist upon a plurality of explanations.... A key word for postmodernism is 'difference'.
>
> (Morgan and Lambert 2005: 54)

School geography has been little influenced by postmodernism so far. League tables and a greater focus on examination results have led to an explosion in the examinations 'industry', by which schools and their students are fed back the rules for success, and, having learned from them, show some hostility towards further change. Meanwhile, academic geography has focused on interconnections of places within a complex and changing world, and there has been an increasing school–HEI 'gap' in the kinds of geography espoused. In human geography in HEI, there is increasing attention given to difference, 'culture', and meanings attached to everyday experiences, to the way places are represented in text, art and film, and how we interpret these, and to environmental issues. There is attention to how we make sense of the world from our particular place within it, and the way this shapes our understanding. Physical geography continues to use scientific approaches, aided by ICT, but there is emphasis on the application of physical geography to problems and on human impact on physical and environmental processes.

Field trips are only now beginning to feel any influence from postmodernism, which has similarly had little influence on geography textbooks and syllabuses. It has influenced topics studied within classrooms, e.g. globalisation, disability or risk, but less on the ways in which they are studied. The Pilot GCSE, which ran from 2001–2008, has lent some influence to the ways that students present and investigate 'place' – e.g. young people's spaces, community space and ownership. The Geographical Association and Royal Geographical Society (with IBG) have together worked on the Action Plan for Geography, particularly to invigorate the subject pre-14. But the overall philosophy or approach has yet to take hold.

Post-14, physical fieldwork remains pseudo-scientific in approach, but human geography has potential to expand its approaches. Some post-16 exam specifications critically investigate themes such as 're-branding', where students are encouraged to use less-formal, subjective and qualitative techniques (e.g. recording by use of photos, interviews). The school geography community is split, however, with most exam boards retaining more traditional data-collection techniques. Coursework post-16 has been lost as a creative influence on fieldwork, and data collection is now embedded in exam specifications in a more formal way.

The potential impacts of 'Learning Outside the Classroom'

Given the shift in paradigms, and the tension between the pedagogies between 'transmissive' and interpretative' teachers, it is almost as if the fieldwork that students will experience depends heavily on the individual preferences and styles of individual teachers and schools. In this sense, government guidance on learning outside the classroom is bound of necessity to be generalised. However, the Manifesto for Learning Outside the Classroom (DfES 2006) highlights four kinds of area in which learning might take place:

- the school grounds;
- the local environment;
- away days;
- residentials.

Each of these environments offer great potential for geographers; if anything, there is perhaps less use of the school grounds and local environment than might be thought, particularly in secondary schools. The local area sometimes holds less attraction for teenage secondary students than distant localities. Nonetheless, there is great potential for using school grounds, from traditional enquiries such as the school micro-climate, to more contemporary, postmodern enquiries about space in school – about identities of different spaces, for instance, or the use of space (e.g. for whom, by whom, and how space usage varies and why).

The manifesto makes big claims for learning outside the classroom. It claims to identify 12 outcomes (Box 10.2) that learning outside can bring, provided it is well planned, safely managed and personalised to meet the needs of every child. However, not all of these can be seen as learning outcomes; at least five of the 12 are either behaviouralist or personal and social. This is not to deny that learning is unaffected by these, but geographers have not always emphasised behaviouralism as a justification for fieldwork, explicitly at least.

Box 10.2 The perceived benefits of Learning Outside the Classroom

Behaviouralist

- Improve young people's attitudes to learning.
- Reduce behaviour problems and improve attendance.
- Stimulate, inspire and improve motivation.

Learning

- Develop active citizens and stewards of the environment.
- Develop skills and independence in a widening range of environments.
- Develop the ability to deal with uncertainty.
- Improve academic achievement.
- Make learning more engaging and relevant to young people.
- Nurture creativity.
- Provide a bridge to higher-order learning.

Personal and social

- Provide challenge and the opportunity to take acceptable levels of risk.
- Provide opportunities for informal learning through play.
  (Source: DfES 2006; categorisation has been done by the author)

For geographers, learning outside the classroom is less problem-free than the manifesto suggests. Indeed, gaining time out of school within term time may actually be becoming more difficult, for a number of reasons:

- Part of the debate about allowing time for fieldwork is that geographers are no longer alone in taking students away from classrooms; other subjects, too, see that as being within their remit. The case for taking students out of class during Years 10–13 is set against increasing demands on school time, particularly as GCSE is changing to modular examination format across all subjects, and goals for both teachers and their students are becoming increasingly short-term. Many geography subject leaders in secondary schools now have to defend their case for what many have previously seen as a birthright.

- Fieldwork and outdoor work are no longer protected by examination specifications, which previously gave subject leaders a perceived right to time out of school; from 2008, coursework was dropped from all post-16 specifications, and from 2009 GCSE specifications use the term 'Controlled Assessment', designed to restrict time spent in fieldwork and the amount of guidance given to students. Although every specification in geography for AS, post-2008, and GCSE, post-2009, continues to state that fieldwork is a requirement, it no longer carries the weight that it did.

- Risk assessment and teachers' legal accountability has created a perceived burden that makes some – perhaps just a few? – teachers hostile towards the administration that field visits entail and therefore to fieldwork itself, be it a half-day trip or a two-week visit to China.

Ofsted's 2008 findings show that learning outside the classroom is no longer the sole preserve of geographers, if it ever was. Their report abounds with examples given from visits organised by teachers of English, maths and science lessons among others; theatre trips are commonplace in schools, and often take place in evenings, treading on fewer curriculum toes in the school day time. In taking students outside class, geographers therefore have to declare their claim upon curriculum time, and to show that it is time well spent. Some of the problem is structural within schools; Ofsted showed that secondary teachers do not often use school *time and space* as flexibly as primary teachers to create opportunities for learning outside the classroom. Perhaps the Manifesto will encourage geography teachers to look closer to home to collaborate with other subject areas. Ofsted found that secondary teachers make much better use of *learning* opportunities than primary, albeit within a narrower subject focus.

Similarly, geographers might do themselves a disservice if they stick rigidly to traditional fieldwork strategies and techniques. With thought and planning, the Manifesto offers plenty of opportunities irrespective of preferred paradigms (Table 10.3). Because of the different paradigms within the subject, there are geographers who overlook the affective domain of learning (see above, Job 1996), for example, in relating to feelings and personal reactions to the environment. In contrast, other teachers have a richness of experience and length of service in teaching students to clarify and justify their own values as a part of geographical enquiry, whilst learning to acknowledge and respect other people's values at the same time. If any geographers doubt the potential of values and affective education, they need only listen to claims made by history teachers, for instance, of the power of taking students to the

Table 10.3 Potential approaches to learning outside the classroom based on different paradigms

Location	Positivist paradigm	Contemporary people–space paradigm
School grounds	Local school micro-climate; investigating patterns of temperature, wind speed etc.	People–space relationships in school – by whom is recreational space used within school? How and why does space usage vary over time of the day, week, term, year?
Local environment	Local employment or services study.	Values enquiry into local controversy or issue, e.g. redevelopment or quality of youth spaces.
Away days	Coastal or river management; assessing a need for management.	Social change and impact of change in an area – e.g. community reactions to London Olympics and Paralympics and regeneration in east London.

Source: *Manifesto for Learning Outside the Classroom* (DfES 2006).

battlefields of the First World War or the sites of former concentration camps of the Second World War; Ofsted cite these as affecting students both emotionally and, in terms of their learning, very effectively.

There are opportunities aplenty provided by the Manifesto. But geographers could claim a degree of irony that the Manifesto was published at a time when their subject and their time was at best under scrutiny, at worst under threat. For geographers, the Manifesto may require an affirmation that fieldwork is what we believe in, and that it is part of our role as geography teachers to develop skills, attitudes and values that arise from learning outside the classroom.

Opportunities for further research

If I have given the impression that fieldwork and work outside the classroom generally has reached a turning point, it is because I believe that there will be ample opportunity for the action researcher in schools to investigate and to assess how work outside the classroom might change in the next decade. Geographers may have to do the – for them – unthinkable in that they may have to justify to a wider audience the central role that they believe fieldwork contributes to the identity of the subject, and the value that it provides – and adds – to students' education.

Dissertation summary

This chapter reflects on two Masters level assignments that both examine fieldwork.

Lindsay Smalldridge (2007) 'To Critically Analyse Teaching in the Field as a Resource for Teaching and Learning'

One fine example of investigation into the effectiveness of fieldwork and the value that it adds, not just to education but to particular students, comes from Lindsay Smalldridge (2007). Her investigation explores the background to fieldwork but adds the dimension of different learning styles. She cites four styles (Table 10.4), from Lambert and Balderstone (2000), which she then uses as a framework against which to assess the effectiveness of different field-work styles in providing for student learning.

Of the traditional field excursion (see above, page 123), she evaluates thus:

> The traditional field excursion is a teacher led fieldwork method, where students are guided through the landscape by their teacher. Auditory learners will learn well as they like listening to the teacher's commentary and deepen their understanding through discussions. Kinaesthetic learners are kept active as they walk, keeping their attention a little longer, if 'the tour is on foot and they have the opportunity to converse with staff' (Kent et al., 1997, p315). Divergers and assimilators like to interpret the landscape and are able to do so in discussions by answering questions posed by the teacher. Assimilators enjoy developing an appreciation of the landscape and nurturing a sense of place, as they like to place their experiences in a theoretical context.

Table 10.4 Some characteristics of different kinds of learner

Accommodators (Dynamic Learners)	Divergers (Imaginative Learners)	Converges (Common-sense Learners)	Assimilators (Analytic Learners)
Characteristics include: • Independent and creative • Likes taking risks and change • Enjoys and adapts well to new situations • Curious and investigative • Inventive, experiments • Problem-solvers	Characteristics include: • Imaginative and creative • Flexible, sees lots of alternatives • Colourful (uses fantasy) • Uses insight • Good at imagining oneself in new/different situations • Uses all senses to interpret	Characteristics include: • Organised, ordered and struc-tured • Practical, 'hands-on' • Detailed and accurate • Applies ideas to solving problems • Learns by testing out new situations and assessing the result • Makes theories useful	Characteristics include: • Logical and structured • Intellectual, academic • Evaluative, good synthesiser • Thinker and debater • Precise, thor-ough, careful • Organised, likes to follow plan • Likes to place experience in theoretical context

Source: adapted from Lambert and Balderstone 2000.

She covers this kind of fieldwork experience positively, and her analysis of enquiry-based fieldwork is thorough, and provides real substance about this style of learning:

> Divergers learn by listening, observing, and then by being given the opportunity to ask their own questions based on their prior background learning.... Accommodators are also very independent and are curious beings that enjoy investigating matters themselves and using their initiative in identifying and gathering relevant information, and enquiry fieldwork gives them the opportunity to do just this. The question, issue or problem to be identified for investigation ideally comes from a student's own experience in the field, and as assimilators look for past experiences in which to extract their learning.... Kinaesthetic and tactile learners will be exposed to practical, hands on activities within the field as they are expected to gather their own appropriate qualitative or quantitative data, providing them a link that stimulates higher order learning.
>
> ... there are some who will be hindered. For example, visual and auditory learners may be discouraged by the lack of input and guidance offered by their teacher, inhibiting the level of understanding they may achieve. Kinaesthetic learners may find the construction of geographical questions through theory work alone daunting and difficult if done independently.

What makes this assignment effective is that it seeks and establishes close relationships between ideas and practice; it leaves her able to see the strengths of each style of learning very effectively. Followed along another path, it would make a substantive base by which to evaluate teaching styles – transmissive or interpretative – and their effectiveness with different learners.

Julius Sidwell (2008) 'Fieldwork in the School Geography Curriculum'

Of great interest is an assignment by Julius Sidwell (2008) who gets straight to the heart of a question that runs through this chapter:

> My question therefore is, are we simply continuing to promote fieldwork within geography due to a historical legacy, or are we promoting it because it is the best use of resources to ensure high quality teaching and learning?

He then analyses the persistence of the excursion and hypothesis testing in school fieldwork:

> Despite the many developments in understanding how to enhance the learning experience of school pupils in the intervening decades, these

strategies have remained steadfastly enshrined in school fieldwork. The question is why this is the case as in many respects (each) flies in the face of modern teaching and learning strategies?

The most powerful line of his argument is when he reflects upon his own experience:

> To put it into context, my school has been inspected this year and it is very clear that inspectors are not impressed by any teacher who simply talks or dictates notes. This does not impress upon inspectors that learning and understanding has taken place. Therefore, how can we promote the use of this strategy through fieldwork when we are trying to suggest to our curriculum managers that it is essential to effective teaching and learning?! The key for me is the pupil reaction to such fieldwork. When given a worksheet, the dominant reaction from many of the pupils is to simply fill in the gaps. This means I would get constantly bombarded with questions such as 'what was the answer to question 4?' or 'what was the last thing you said sir?' They are not asking geographical questions. They see their task for the day as one of filling in the gaps or copying down what I say.

For discussion

Sidwell's questions provide a good opportunity to draw together some questions that will prove worthy of exploration:

- What is the unique contribution made by working outside the classroom to students' learning?
- At a time when virtual fieldwork is being promoted via Google Maps and some sophisticated GIS packages, what contribution will they, too, make to geographical learning?
- Will the absence of individualised investigations post-16 create a 'different' kind of fieldwork? Will students now be taken to 'look and see', or to investigate examples of what they have studied? Or will fieldwork prove as truly investigative as it has in the previous three decades? What implications will this have for enquiry-based work post-16? Similarly, how far will 'Controlled Assessment' act as a stimulus for, or a brake upon, creatively designed fieldwork for students at GCSE?
- How far will either of these changes post-14 and post-16 promote or prevent residential fieldwork?
- How far will school or administrative (rather than learning or curriculum) factors influence the kinds of work done by students in the 14–18 age range outside the classroom? Will there be an insistence that students can only travel a certain distance? Or visit sites only within day trips?

As Julius Sidwell observes, there are some hard questions for geographers to face up to.

Further reading

1 Barnes, Douglas (1976) *From Communication to Curriculum.* Harmondsworth: Penguin. Over 30 years old and it provides clear, readable insight about how and why teachers differ. The basis of so much research about the role of teachers, learners, and language and learning in the classroom.
2 Kent, A., Lambert, D., Naish, M. and Slater, F. (ed.) (1996) *Geography in Education.* Cambridge: Cambridge University Press. An excellent reader about the role of geography in education, with lasting commentaries about the growing HEI–school divide and explorations of paradigms in the subject. Includes a brilliant chapter by David Job, referenced within the text.
3 Walford, R. (2001) *Geography in British Schools 1850–2000.* London: Woburn Press. This provides an excellent basis for tracing the paradigm shifts, and how these were made manifest in British schools.

References

Barnes, Douglas (1976) *From Communication to Curriculum.* Harmondsworth: Penguin.
Bruner, J. (1966) *Towards a Theory of Instruction.* New York: Norton.
Butt, G. (2000) *The Continuum Guide to Geography Education.* London: Continuum.
DfES (2006) *Learning Outside the Classroom.* London: HMSO.
Digby, Bob (2008) *Teaching A Level Geography.* A Think Piece published by the Geographical Association, Sheffield. Online, available at: www.geography.org.uk. *With acknowledgment to Margaret Roberts as editor for her contribution to the discussion about geographical paradigms.*
Goudie, A. (1994) 'The nature of physical geography: a view from the drylands', *Geography* 79/3: 194–209.
Job, David (1996) 'Geography and environmental education – an exploration of perspectives and strategies', in Kent, A., Lambert, D., Naish, M. and Slater, F. (eds) *Geography in Education.* Cambridge: Cambridge University Press.
Johnston, R., Gregory, D., Pratt, G. and Watts, M. (eds) (2000) *The Dictionary of Human Geography, 4th edition.* Oxford: Blackwell.
Lambert, D. and Balderstone, D. (2000) *Learning to Teach Geography in the Secondary School.* London: Routledge.
Morgan, J. and Lambert, D. (2005) *Geography: Teaching School Subjects 11–19.* London: Routledge.
Naish, Michael, Rawling, Eleanor and Hart, Clive (1987) *Geography 16-19: the Contribution Of A Curriculum Project To 16–19 Education.* Harlow: Longman.
Ofsted (2008) *Geography in Schools: Changing Practice.* Office for Standards in Education.
Unwin, T. (1992) *The Place of Geography.* Harlow: Longman.
Valentine, G. (2001) *Social Geographies: Space and Society.* Harlow: Prentice Hall.

Part III

Writing and researching geography education

11 Engaging with theory

Denise Freeman

For many teachers, the notion of engaging with theory may seem like an additional burden on their time; a distraction from the 'real-world' of teaching and learning. However, it can be argued that theory and theoretical understanding lie at the heart of what goes on in the classroom. By engaging with theory it is possible to understand how we have got where we are today. Moreover, by critiquing theory it is possible to consider alternative ways forward and help shape the future of teaching and learning. The focus of this chapter is to encourage teachers to 'unpack' their personal theoretical understanding(s) and show how engaging with theory can be a useful and important aspect of teaching and learning in the geography classroom.

The aims of this chapter are:

- to help teachers make links between theory and practice.
- to consider some of the practical applications of theories about learning, curriculum and geography.
- to explore how engaging with theory and theoretical debate can help teachers to ask 'big' questions about geography education.

This chapter focuses on theories in both education and geography. It can be argued that educational theory falls into two main areas. The first includes theories about the way in which students learn: learning theory. The second concerns the way in which learning is approached and organised: curriculum theory. These two 'categories' should not been seen as mutually exclusive, as they are strongly connected and interlinked. For example, it is suggested by Moore (2000) that Piaget's theories of learning and child development have had a strong influence on the way in which the National Curriculum in the UK is organised.

Learning theory

Many of the theorists who have contributed to the field of learning theory are very well known. For example, Piaget, Vygotsky and Bruner are names that most teachers are familiar with (see Moore 2000 for a useful summary of

the contributions made by these key theorists). However, whilst most teachers have explored learning theory at some point during their training or
further study, they may not always be consciously aware of how such theories
relate to their daily practice in the classroom (Moore 2000).

This link between theory and practice is explored by Roberts (2003) in
her work on enquiry learning. Focusing mostly on the work of Vygotsky
(1962), Roberts argues that learning theory underpins many of the concepts
and processes involved in geographical enquiry. Central to her discussion is
Vygotsky's concept of the 'zone of proximal development' (ZPD); the gap
between what someone can do unaided and what they can do with help and
support. Roberts argues that according to Vygotskian theory, effective geographical enquiry should challenge students and take them 'beyond what they
can already do' (2003: 29). Furthermore, teachers should support students
with geographical enquiry work and the tasks set should not take them
beyond their limits (outside of their ZPD), but be appropriately challenging.

Roberts (2003) shows how engaging with learning theory can prompt
teachers to ask complex questions that get to the heart of the learning experience. For example, is support something provided exclusively by teachers or
can support come from other, maybe older, students?

In addition, theories can cause contradictions. For example, Vygotsky's
work appears to challenge the idea of students working totally independently
on enquiry work (Roberts 2003). Yet, independent learning is something
widely considered to be an important skill that should be encouraged in
schools. It is also something that is often demanded of students during enquiry
work outside school, e.g. at home. This poses questions about how students
can be encouraged to take effective ownership of their own learning in geography (both inside the classroom and beyond) and if independent learning
can sufficiently challenge students.

Roberts' discussion of the links between geographical enquiry and Vygotsky's writing exemplifies the relevance of theory to a familiar aspect of geographical education. Moreover, it suggests that by looking critically at theory
and asking questions, teachers can begin to 'unpack' their practice and reflect
upon the learning taking place in the classroom.

Curriculum theory

In very general terms, curriculum theory tends to focus upon what is taught
in schools and why (Kliebard 1999). For early curriculum theorists, 'the' curriculum was something that could be analysed scientifically. These theorists
believed that science and scientific methods could be used to establish what
should be taught in schools and how educational knowledge should be constructed (Scott 2008). During the 1960s and 1970s a more 'analytical understanding of the socially situated nature of curriculum developed' (Moon and
Murphy 1999: 1) and curriculum theorists began to explore the ways in
which the curriculum can be seen as socially, politically and culturally

constructed. The school curriculum, then, reflects the variety of social, political and cultural interests of those involved in education; from those working in the classroom to policy-makers and politicians.

Recently, a number of commentators have expressed concern that theoretical debate about the nature of the school curriculum is in decline. Drawing on the work of Bernstein, an influential curriculum theorist, Scott (2008) argues that most governments around the world appear to have reached a 'settlement about the nature of the school curriculum'. He argues that a 'false consensus on curriculum, barely agreed and certainly not negotiated, has replaced what was once a vigorous debate about … the curriculum' (2008: 5). Teachers have also not been engaging with curriculum. Morgan and Lambert (2005: 40) argue that, in the case of geography, emphasis has been placed upon encouraging teachers to examine '*how to teach* rather than *what to teach* or [even] *why teach geography*'.

Applying theory to practice

The process of selecting which course students follow at GCSE or post-16 level is a useful example of the way in which these theoretical questions may arise in the classroom. Choosing an exam specification is an important decision faced by teachers and subject leaders. There are several different exam specifications for geography, run by various exam boards. Each exam specification reflects particular elements of learning and curriculum theory, as well as different approaches to the subject. Furthermore, the choices made by teachers are influenced by their own personal 'take' on such theories.

What follows is a brief examination of some of the theoretical questions that arise when analysing the GCSE geography specifications on offer to schools in England and Wales. Table 11.1 provides an overview of the main GCSE geography exam specifications 'on the market'.

In order to 'market' their course(s), each awarding body publishes promotional literature that is sent out to schools, along with the detailed specification. Quotes from this literature are included in Table 11.1. Analysis of these quotes highlights a tendency for exam boards to offer two contrasting specifications; one that is seen as more 'traditional' and one that is seen as 'new' or, in the case of AQA B, 'innovative'. 'Traditional' courses enable teachers to work with an existing view of what school geography is, whilst those that are marketed as 'new' offer alternative constructions of the subject. But where do these constructions come from? Who has made the decision to include these 'new' elements of geography in the curriculum and why? Furthermore, why do some parts of 'traditional' school geography remain in the specifications (e.g. rivers, coasts, population and settlement, in the case of AQA A), whilst others have been removed? And who is involved in the selection process?

A further point for consideration by teachers is how each specification views geography as a discipline. For example, those promoting the Edexcel A course explain that 'fundamental concepts' will be covered by the course. Meanwhile, the WJEC A course has an entire unit entitled 'core geography'.

Table 11.1 Summary of 2009 GCSE Geography Exam Specifications

Awarding body	Specification	What the awarding body says	Content (for full courses)
AQA	A	'Familiar content' 'Traditional structure' 'Will make geography even more relevant and innovating for . . . students.'	**Unit 1:** Physical Geography **Unit 2:** Human Geography **Unit 3:** Controlled Assessment (Local Fieldwork Investigation)
AQA	B	'A more innovative look at the subject' 'No core content – all the content is optional.'	**Unit 1:** Managing Places in the 21st Century **Unit 2:** Hostile World **Unit 3:** Investigating the Shrinking World **Unit 4:** Controlled Assessment (Local Fieldwork Investigation and Geographical Issue Investigation)
OCR	A	'Lively and innovative, based on a successful 3 year pilot' Promotes the use of 'up-to-date' technologies, and topics that reflect the real world, . . .' '[captures] the imagination and interest of you and your learners.' It is 'at the forefront of developing qualifications for the 21st century.' 'We embrace innovation in developing specification which bring the subject to life for their pupils.'	**Unit A671:** Extreme Environments **Unit A672:** You as a global citizen – the impact of our decisions **Unit A673:** Similarities and Differences **Unit A674:** Issues in our fast changing world
OCR	B	'Mostly built around the popular existing qualifications; Geography A, Avery Hill and Bristol Project.' 'A balance of theoretical and practical work encourages an active involvement in the subject, . . .' 'This familiar, quality specification has been updated to reflect modern geography.' 'aims to enthuse and stimulate interest amongst learners . . .'	**Unit B561:** Sustainable Decision Making **Unit B562:** Geographical Enquiry **Unit B563:** Key Geographical Themes

Edexcel	A	'Exciting specification covering the subject's **fundamental concepts** with more exciting topic choice.' 'the number of case studies has been reduced, … the emphasis now on understanding geographical processes rather than the locational detail [often] used to illustrate those processes.' 'Traditional areas such as rivers, coasts, population and settlement … have been enriched by adding material about the problems posed by different environments and how they might be best managed.'	**Unit 1:** Geographical Skills and Challenges (Section A: Geographical Skills, Section B: Challenges for the Planet) **Unit 2:** The Natural Environment (Section A: The Physical Environment, Section B: Environmental Issues) **Unit 3:** The Human Environment (Section A: The Human World, Section B: People Issues) **Unit 4:** Investigating Geography
Edexcel	B	A 'contemporary, **issues-based** specification using geographical concepts to explain key issues facing today's world, …' 'Flexible and more exciting four-unit assessment structure with a greater choice of optional units, helping you to personalise the course.'	**Unit 1:** Dynamic Planet **Unit 2:** People and Planet **Unit 3:** Making Geographical Decisions **Unit 4:** Researching Geography
WJEC	A	'a clear balance between physical and human themes …' and a balance 'between the more traditional themes of geography and the more contemporary themes …' '… a desire to challenge students to consider their role in society and their part in creating positive geographical futures …'	**Unit 1:** Core Geography **Unit 2:** Options Geography **Unit 3:** Geographical Enquiry
WJEC	B (Avery Hill)* *The course is managed jointly by WJEC and OCR	'has the highest entry figures for GCSE Geography in the UK.' 'An issue based, investigative approach to geography is at the core of each unit.' Students 'will be able to widen and deepen their own views whist appreciating the complexity and range of views held by others'.	**Unit 1:** Challenges and Interactions in Geography **Unit 2:** Development and Problem Solving in Geography **Unit 3:** Geographical Enquiry

This language implies the existence of 'core' elements of geography; it is suggested that these core elements are 'fixed' and help make geography what it is. This view sits well with the theories of those who see curriculum development as a scientific process. In contrast, a number of specifications (e.g. AQA (A & B) and Edexcel B) emphasise the absence of 'core' content, highlighting the degree of content choice given to teachers. Table 11.1 only provides an overview of the *main* units of work featured on each specification; many units are broken down into smaller sections using sub-headings. Unit titles say a great deal about the view of geography being presented by each specification. For example, some specifications divide geography into two key areas of study, human geography and physical geography; a more 'traditional' view of the discipline. For teachers, the choice of exam specification will reflect their own theories on geographical content, curriculum and their local context.

Other specifications use more contemporary, 'exciting' language in their titles, e.g. 'Dynamic Planet' or 'Hostile World'. These titles could be seen as an attempt to engage students and make geography 'relevant'. However, it is important to consider where these titles come from, what geographical content they contain and to what extent it is innovative? These questions enable teachers to get at the heart of the reasons for their choice of examination specification and are fundamental to the type of geographical learning they wish to emphasise.

Asking 'big' questions about school geography

> Geography,
> What are you?
> What makes you?
> Whose knowledge do you represent?
> Whose reality do you reflect?
> > (An extract from 'An Ode to Geography' from Clare Madge,
> > *Feminist Geographies: Explorations in Diversity and Difference* by the WGSG,
> > Pearson 1997)

The analysis of exam specifications, found in the previous section of this chapter, demonstrated how theory can help us to question the practice of teaching and learning geography in schools. 'Big' questions are also raised by Clare Madge (in the extract above), in which she questions the very nature of geography. The following section of this chapter illustrates how engaging with theory and theoretical debate about school geography can help teachers to explore some of these 'big' questions.

What is school geography?

In her 'Ode to Geography', Madge (WGSG 1997) questions what geography is. For some educational philosophers (for example, Hirst 1974; quoted in

Morgan and Lambert 2005: 75) the answer lays in 'natural laws' or 'ways of knowing' about our planet which need to be discovered and understood, in order to explain what we see around us. According to such theorists, geography helps us to uncover these laws and gain knowledge about how the world works. Constructivists disagree with this view, claiming that geography and geographical knowledge are not given entities; instead they have been socially constructed.

For constructivists, our knowledge of the world is shaped by a variety of social, cultural and political views, interests and ideologies. In the case of school geography, knowledge has been constructed by a variety of interest groups including curriculum planners, teachers, textbook writers and those involved in PGCE courses (Huckle 2002). Roberts argues that school geography can be seen as a product of people asking 'particular questions ... at particular times and in particular places' (2003: 28). Furthermore, it is argued by some that those asking the questions and making the decisions belong to more powerful groups in society (Huckle 2002; Morgan and Lambert 2005).

The view that geographical knowledge and school geography are socially constructed has implications for the curriculum, particularly if the curriculum is seen as a text, written and constructed by a certain group of people at a certain time. Viewing the curriculum in this way suggests that 'geography teachers are not teaching knowledge but preferred [or chosen] discourses' (Lambert and Balderstone 2000: 35). These discourses are not fixed; instead they develop and change over time.

It is certainly useful for teachers then to have some understanding of the historical development of school geography (for example see Walford 2000). However, such texts have been criticised for their emphasis on the chronological and uncritical account of the evolution of geography in schools (Ploszajska 2000; quoted in Morgan 2002: 26). In an attempt to address this issue, commentators have sought to analyse the social, political and cultural processes involved in the process of constructing school geography (see Huckle 2002; Morgan 2002; Morgan and Lambert 2005; Rawling 2001). Whilst this development has been welcomed by many, Heffernan (2003; quoted in Morgan and Lambert 2005: 7) argues that it remains important for readers to question '*whose* history' of the subject is being presented, and by implication whose are not.

What emerges from examining the historical development of the curriculum is that the aims and approaches of school geography have altered over time. As such, the 'definition' of school geography is continually shifting. This process of change is led in part by official curriculum documents and policy documents, but is also influenced by textbooks and educational resources.

An example of how and why the content of the curriculum may change is provided by examining the schemes of work published by QCA in 2000. These schemes of work were aimed at helping teachers to deliver the Curriculum 2000. The schemes of work for Key Stage 3 geography included topics such as 'Crime and the Community', 'The Geography of Sport' and 'The Geography of Fashion'. These units of work were seen to present 'new', modern geographies that are relevant to young people in schools (Morgan and Lambert 2005). The schemes of work published by QCA were also supported by new textbooks and other publications. In some ways, the schemes of work became the new curriculum. However, it can be argued that by simply accepting these units of work as being 'what school geography is' teachers avoided asking important theoretical questions. Such questions include 'why have these units been included?', 'who has created them?' and 'what is their purpose'?

Another example of the need to ask theoretical questions about *what* is being taught in geography is provided by Standish (2007). Writing about the growing inclusion of global citizenship education and global ethics in the geography curriculum, Standish (2007: 29) accuses geographers of jumping on the 'internationalisation bandwagon' and re-inventing geography as 'a subject that teaches students about these "new" global processes and issues'. He argues that this has been done 'with no critical interrogation of the education and social implications of these concepts' (Standish 2007: 29). Standish claims that rather than 'teaching pupils about the world so that they can decide the most appropriate course of action' (something that he believes has been a long tradition in school geography); global citizenship education is replacing 'knowledge with morality as the central focus of the curriculum' (2007: 39).

In a review of Standish's writing, Lambert (2008: 183) argues that Standish is making the case against a school geography that simply teaches students 'how to behave' and how to 'save the world'. Lambert sees this as an important contribution to the debate about *what* geography is for and *how* decisions are made about the geography curriculum.

How is the world represented through school geography?

In this chapter, I have explored the relevance of theory to teachers of school geography. This engagement with theory may lead teachers to question the way in which the world around us is represented in the classroom.

According to constructivist theory, our knowledge of the world is socially and culturally constructed. Roberts (2003: 28) argues that geographers and geography educators have developed 'ways of seeing the world' and have constructed theories to understand it. It is for teachers to question how this is represented in school geography – and in particular how young people learn about the world around them.

In the past, geographers have focused upon a 'fixed' view of the world, 'external to the observer' and accessible through the use of 'appropriate methods' (Lambert and Balderstone 2000: 34). This 'scientific view' has been challenged with recent geographical theorists tending to see the world as a 'text'; a text that has been written by many people and that can be read and interpreted in a multitude of different ways (Lambert and Balderstone 2000: 34). Enabling students to access different readings of this 'text' is an important challenge for geography teachers (see Bermingham *et al.* 1999).

The way in which the world and 'distant' places are represented through school geography is an issue explored by Langton (2005) in his study of student perceptions of developing countries. In particular, he highlights the way in which GCSE and A-level exam boards view development issues and include them in their curriculum documents. Langton's work is discussed in detail in the dissertation summary that follows.

Dissertation summary

Richard Langton (2005) 'An Investigation into Perceptions and Attitudes Towards Developing Countries in Secondary Geography Education'

Langton's research explores how and why student perceptions of developing countries change as they move through the different stages of secondary education. Langton aims to 'look towards a sense of best practice that all schools can follow in incorporating global citizenship and, in particular, the situation and future of developing countries'. He also attempts 'to challenge stereotypes and the way in which students view other people'. This dissertation has been chosen to accompany this chapter because it explores some of the dominant discourses of development education and highlights the way in which they have featured on the geography curriculum. This is a good example of a teacher questioning *what* is included in the curriculum, and *how* students can learn effectively about development issues.

In his literature review Langton discusses different definitions of development. He also provides a historical perspective on international development, with particular consideration given to how the development of a country may be measured. Langton argues that issues of economic and social development are highly complex; complicated by issues of corruption, war, poverty, world trade and investment by multinational corporations. Langton goes on to consider the implications this complexity has for development education. He outlines some of the principles of development education and discusses the establishment of relevant agencies aimed at supporting teachers in the classroom. Langton also highlights the growing importance of citizenship and sustainability within schools, and highlights their relevance to development education.

In the latter stages of his literature review, Langton discusses different approaches to development education, outlining various national and local projects aimed at challenging common stereotypes of those living in developing countries, and enhancing student understanding of life in 'distant places'. Langton concludes his literature review by stating that the central premise of development education should be to help students to 'understand the links between their own lives and those of people throughout the world [through an] understanding of the economic, social, political and environmental forces which shape them' (www.dea.org.uk/schools; quoted in Langton 2005: 31).

Langton also analyses the way in which development education features on the national curriculum and in GCSE and A-level courses. He provides a critical overview of the guidance and 'prescription' given to teachers in the form of the National Curriculum, QCA schemes of work and course sylla-buses at KS4/5. Langton concludes that 'there is substantial opportunity for students to develop an appreciation of development and global citizenship' at all stages of secondary education, but he questions whether teachers are taking these opportunities and what degree of influence they have on student per-ceptions of developing countries (2005: 46).

Having established that there is 'plenty of opportunity for teachers to explore the key strands of development education through the available cur-riculum/syllabuses ...', Langton goes on to investigate student perceptions of developing countries through a survey of over 400 students across Key Stage 3, 4 and 5. Included in this sample were over 100 students who had experi-enced or were due to experience developing countries first-hand through an organisation called World Challenge. The results of the survey are analysed in detail. Langton concludes that distinct differences were found in the views of students from different schools and of different ages. Furthermore, student opinions are 'mainly influenced by topics and examples they have studied in class' (2005: 71). Langton argues that this 'represents the influence [that] teachers have in structuring the thought processes and level of citizenship within students' (2005: 71).

Having conducted a school-based survey of student perceptions of devel-oping countries, Langton then contrasts his findings with those gathered from students who had visited a developing country as part of the World Challenge programme. Students were surveyed on their perceptions before and after their visit. The responses of the students that had taken part in a month-long trip to a developing country 'were markedly different from all those who had filled in the questionnaires previously' (2005: 79). Their definitions of what a developing country is were 'more sympathetic, focussing on why countries were held back (e.g. by debt or poor infrastructures) rather than simple iden-tifying them as being poorer' (2005: 79). Langton argues that the students who had taken part in the visits were given 'a unique opportunity ... to experience developing countries, to challenge their own perceptions and to develop new skills' (2005: 80).

In the conclusion to his study, Langton argues that 'development educa-tion *is* available to all' and that 'there are an increasing amount of resources and opportunities available to teachers in order to give students a balanced viewpoint about life in developing countries' (2005: 91). Langton also high-lights the importance of questioning stereotypes and unpacking perceptions of distant places and developing countries. He makes a case for development education that allows young people 'to talk to each other and adults in order to challenge their own thinking' (2005: 91). For Langton, a wide variety of opportunities are available for teachers involved in development education and he urges geography teachers to explore them.

Langton's research is valuable as it raises many questions about the way in which views of international development and development education have changed and evolved over time. It provides a comprehensive overview of how development issues are presented to teachers and students through the National Curriculum and exam syllabuses. Furthermore, Langton raises important questions about how what students learn in school can have a strong influence in shaping their perceptions of people and places.

For discussion

Below is a list of critical questions aimed at helping teachers to make connections between some of the theories discussed in this chapter and their classroom practice.

* What curriculum models appear to be dominant in your school and/or in your department?
* What makes geography 'distinct' as a school subject in your school and/ in your classroom?
* What links are made between geography and other areas of the curriculum?
* How can teachers be given opportunities to effectively engage with theory?

The following questions provide stimulus for further research into the development of the 2009 GCSE geography exam specifications:

* How does QCA set the criteria that exam boards must follow when developing a new course? Who and what shapes this criteria?
* What influence do these criteria have on the content of the specifications?
* To what extent can these 'new' specifications be seen as 'new' constructions? In what ways do previous specifications continue to shape the curriculum?
* What role do unit titles have to play in shaping student views of the world?
* What role do economic and political factors play in curriculum development? For example, how can we explain the emphasis placed upon ICT and GIS in the 'new' specifications?

Further reading

1 Moore, A. (2000) *Teaching and Learning: Pedagogy, Curriculum and Culture*. London: RoutledgeFalmer. This book provides a very useful and accessible introduction to theory and issues of pedagogy and curriculum.

2 Morgan, J. and Lambert, D. (2005) *Teaching School Subjects: Geography (Teaching School Subjects 11–19)*. London: RoutledgeFalmer. This book provides a highly valuable and contemporary overview of issues in geography education. It provides a great deal of stimulus for reflection and research.
3 Rawling, E. (2001) *Changing the Subject: the Impact of National Policy on School Geography 1980 – 2000*. Sheffield: The Geographical Association. This book provides a very thorough, valuable and critical overview of the introduction of the National Curriculum in the UK. It is an important reference point for those wishing to place curriculum theory in context.
4 Scott, D. (2008) *Critical Essays on Major Curriculum Theorists*. Abingdon: Routledge. This book provides a detailed and critical analysis of curriculum theory. It has contributions from ten influential curriculum theorists including Jerome Bruner and Basil Bernstein.

Note

Information about exam specifications can be obtained from the websites of the respective examination boards.

References

Bermingham, S., Slater, F. and Yangopoulos, S. (1999) 'Multiple Texts, Alternative Texts, Multiple Readings, Alternative Readings', *Teaching Geography* 24, 4, 160–168.
Cloke, P., Crang, P. and Goodwin, M. (1999) *Introducing Human Geographies*. London: Arnold.
Heffernan, M. (2003) 'Histories of Geography', in S. Holloway, S. Rice and G. Valentine (eds) *Key Concepts in Geography*. London: Sage, pp. 3–22.
Hirst, P.H. (1974) *Knowledge and the Curriculum: a Collection of Philosophical Papers*. London: Routledge.
Huckle, J. (2002) 'Towards a Critical School Geography', in M. Smith (ed.) *Teaching Geography in Secondary Schools*. London: RoutledgeFalmer, pp. 255–265.
Kliebard, H. (1999) 'Constructing the Concept of Curriculum on the Wisconsin Frontier: How Social Restructuring Sustained a Pedagogical Revolution', in B. Moon and P. Murphey (eds) *Curriculum in Context*. London: Paul Chapman.
Lambert, D. (2008) 'Review Article: the Corruption of the Curriculum', *Geography* 93, 3, pp. 183–185.
Lambert, D. and Balderstone, D. (2000) *Learning to Teach Geography in the Secondary School*. London: RoutledgeFalmer.
Langton, R. (2005) *An Investigation into Perceptions and Attitudes Towards Developing Countries in Secondary Geography Education*. Unpublished dissertation, Institute of Education.
Moon, B. and Murphey, P. (1999) *Curriculum in Context*. London: Paul Chapman.
Moore, A. (2000) *Teaching and Learning: Pedagogy, Curriculum and Culture*. London: RoutledgeFalmer.
Morgan, J. (2002) 'Constructing School Geographies', in M. Smith (ed.) *Teaching Geography in Secondary Schools*. London: RoutledgeFalmer, pp. 40–59.
Morgan, J. and Lambert, D. (2005) *Teaching School Subjects: Geography (Teaching School Subjects 11–19*. London: RoutledgeFalmer.

Ploszajska, T. (2000) 'Historiographies of Geography and Empire', in B. Graham and C. Nash (eds) *Modern Historical Geographies*. London: Prentice Hall, pp. 121–145.

Rawling, E. (2001) *Changing the Subject: the Impact of National Policy on School Geography 1980 – 2000*. Sheffield: the Geographical Association.

Roberts, M. (2003) *Learning Through Enquiry*. Sheffield: The Geographical Association.

Scott, D. (2008) *Critical Essays on Major Curriculum Theorists*. Abingdon: Routledge.

Standish, A. (2007) 'Geography Used to be About Maps', in R. Whelan (ed.) *The Corruption of the Curriculum*. London: Civitas, pp. 28–57.

Vygotsky, L. (1962) *Thought and Language*. Cambridge, MA: MIT Press.

Walford, R. (2000) *Geography in British Schools 1850–2000*. London: Woburn Press.

Women and Geography Study Group (WGSG) (1997) *Feminist Geographies: Explorations in Diversity and Difference*. Pearson.

12 Undertaking research and doing a dissertation

Clare Brooks, Adrian Conradi and Alison Leonard

There is currently a push in the UK for teachers to acquire Masters level qualifications in order to make teaching a Masters level profession (see Introduction). This means that more geography teachers may now consider undertaking post-graduate research and a dissertation as part of Masters level studies. For many teachers this may be the first time they undertake research at this level or into a practical professional activity like teaching. The main aim of this chapter is to offer some inspiration and a starting point for geography teachers considering undertaking a dissertation or research at this level.

The aims of this chapter are:

- to reflect on the value of undertaking research, particularly a dissertation, both personally and professionally.
- to consider what a dissertation is and what undertaking one involves.
- to offer some practical advice on how to go about the process of selecting and undertaking your dissertation topic.

This chapter is structured into three parts. In the first part, Clare Brooks gives an overview of some important principles to consider when undertaking the research process. In the second part, Adrian Conradi gives a personal account of his experience of undertaking and completing his dissertation research for the MA in Geography Education (at the Institute of Education, University of London). In the third part, Alison Leonard explores research at Masters level and some of the benefits to come out of it, using David Mitchell's research into a curriculum development project as an example.

Writing a dissertation

In 1996, Ashley Kent reflected on how tutors on the MA in Geography Education (at the IOE) supported their tutees through the research process. The categories identified in Kent's chapter are as relevant now as they were then (see Box 12.1). Kent's advice and guidance shows the pitfalls of undertaking research at this level, but there are also key principles that can help to facilitate the process which the first part of this chapter will address. It is also worth noting (as Conradi does later in this chapter — see page 155) that technology can facilitate the research process, but cannot replace the thinking and decision-making that can make undertaking research at this level so rewarding.

Box 12.1 Key events of undertaking Masters level research (taken from Kent 1996)

- Finding a focus
- Deciding on the right approach to take
- Reading around the topic
- Making and meeting deadlines
- Starting to write
- Tutorial support.

Clarity

The first key principle is clarity. Many researchers struggle to pin down the exact nature of their enquiry in the early stages of research, and Kent observes that there is some benefit to starting with a broad focus. This is wise advice, as often the research process does not proceed as planned. However, having a clear idea of what the research is about is an extremely useful starting point and one that is worth spending time developing. Having identified a topic or area that you would like to research, the difficulty is to narrow down what it is about that topic that you wish to find out.

In my experience, a researcher can encounter two pitfalls here. One is the 'hunch'. In this category, the research starts out as an observation or 'hunch' that the researcher wishes to share or prove. The 'hunch' could be well-grounded in their practical experience. There may even be some readings to support it. In many ways a hunch can be useful as the research focus can be relatively clear. The pitfall, however, is in the integrity of the research. Having identified their hunch, the challenge for the researcher is to develop a research methodology that enables them to also explore their interpretation of the hunch alongside alternative explanations or possibilities. The researcher has to demonstrate that they are open to different points of view and evidence that may disprove their hunch.

The second pitfall is where the researcher has a general area of interest, but is finding it difficult to narrow down precisely what they wish to research. In this situation, reading relevant research is useful. This can help the researcher to eliminate areas that have already been researched and to identify gaps where research has not been conducted. In this scenario, undertaking the review of relevant literature can help to narrow down the research focus and in refining the research questions.

Whichever way the researcher arrives at their research questions, they must also be clear and precise. Tutors are useful here to give feedback, question assumptions and to identify any vague areas. Most researchers find their research questions valuable throughout the research to keep it on track and to help them reflect on issues and tensions along the way.

Knowing about research processes

Another principle that emerges from Kent's chapter is the need for a detailed understanding of the process of research. Research is often fraught with logistical and theoretical difficulties. When researching with others, carefully worked out schedules can be disrupted through illness and unexpected changes. Logistical difficulties are inevitable parts of the research process and will affect the research. The rigorous researcher will make their decisions explicit, and will have thought-through the methodological implications of the decisions they make.

Researching involves resolving complex theoretical questions. These can be ethical in nature: for instance, if previous research suggests that a certain approach can benefit students, is it ethical to undertake an experiment where some students are not given this advantage? The questions may be fundamental to what is being studied. For instance, my recent research looked at the practice of 'expert' geography teachers. Throughout my research I questioned what was meant by expertise in education. I asked questions: is it important for others to share my understanding of expertise? How do I know if someone is an expert? Does an expert geography teacher have to be expert in all areas of geography and/or teaching?

Similarly, questions may arise as to what can be known. For instance, if a researcher is examining the effectiveness of an assessment strategy, and gets a positive outcome from an intervention, they need to question if the results are related to the intervention. Interviewing is especially tricky here: does the researcher know that what the respondent says is what they really think, or if they are merely saying what they think is 'right' or what the researcher wants to hear?

The distinction between ontology (what the world is actually like) and epistemology (what we can know about the world) is useful here. Most early researchers start out wanting to find out about what the world is really like, but end up realising that their research is more about what can be known. This is a subtle but important difference, and may mean that in dissertations, sentences do not state: 'therefore this strategy works' but state 'therefore in this instance, there was a positive outcome'. This difference acknowledges that the specific context may influence both the research design and outcomes.

Understanding the nature of education research also means understanding how your research stands amongst previous research and what it adds to the debate. It can be tempting to think that positive results from research will apply to other contexts. Many researchers describe the process of undertaking research as a transformative experience. It is understandable, therefore, that these researchers are convinced that others will be able to benefit from their findings. And, of course, research can be very beneficial to others – but with some reservations. Every teacher, class and lesson has unique features. Much research is sensitive to this uniqueness, and so caution must be exercised in describing the generalisability of the research findings. Just because something 'works' in your research doesn't mean that it is generalisable to all contexts (Bassey's description of fuzzy generalisations (1999) are useful here).

There are many useful texts on the research and dissertation-writing process (see recommended reading section at the end of this chapter). But nothing replaces personal experience, and hence below Adrian Conradi shares his dissertation journey.

My dissertation

Adrian Conradi

In order to put this chapter into some context, I will start off by introducing myself and my own dissertation journey.

Biographical detail

I undertook my Masters in Geography Education after eight years of teaching. Undertaking a Masters degree was an ambition of mine to challenge myself and expand career options and I spent a long time choosing the right course for me. I wanted a Masters programme that suited my personal and professional needs whilst also providing the intellectual challenge that I associated with Masters work. Ultimately I wanted to learn more about my work and therefore undertaking a dissertation was an important part of this process of learning and critical self-reflection.

Although my professional context is quite unusual, it provided a perfect platform upon which to base my dissertation focus. I teach Canadian curriculum geography in a private school in China. My students are Chinese and have studied a Chinese curriculum for nine years before entering one ESOL (English for speakers of other languages) intensive year followed by a three-year Canadian (British Columbia) secondary graduation programme. The geography course that I teach is not as popular as other subjects and there is an impression among the students that it is difficult. In grades 10 and 11 of the Canadian programme, the students also take some Chinese curriculum classes, including Chinese geography. One of the Chinese geography teachers at the school took an interest in how geography is taught in the Canadian classes and started attending my classes. Over a period of two years, we developed a relationship based on discussions on what problems our students face, the students' perception of geography, and how we might be able to cooperate to enhance learning and improve their achievement in my course. The relationship with my

Chinese colleague (and our cooperative efforts to address the above-mentioned issues) developed into what I came to term a 'Cross Cultural Teaching Team'. This seemed to be a natural topic for my dissertation.

Therefore, for me, selecting my dissertation topic was quite straight-forward. However, considering the purpose and value of the dissertation was an important initial step in clarifying what I was doing a dissertation (and ultimately a Masters degree) for.

I was able to settle on three research questions that directly related to my professional challenge in the geography classroom:

- What is the progression in geographical knowledge/understanding/skills between the Chinese-programme geography and the Canadian-programme geography?
- Are there areas of the Canadian-programme geography that are of particular difficulty for offshore school students?
- Are there specific ways that Cross Cultural Teaching Teams (CCTTs) can support student learning and achievement in Canadian-programme geography?

These research goals were achieved through a mixed approach, combining quantitative and qualitative methods that included:

- textbook analysis;
- test-result analysis;
- interviews with students and the Chinese geography teacher;
- observation and personal reflection.

My findings indicate that significant areas of difficulty exist for offshore students studying Canadian-curriculum geography, but suggest some of these may be overcome via Cross Cultural Teaching Teams. An outcome of my dissertation was a model to represent our Cross Cultural Teaching Team (see Box 12.2).

Box 12.2 Example of a usable product that a dissertation may produce

Steps to take when establishing a Cross Cultural Teaching Team

1   Determine if there is a need for a CCTT.
   - Are there problems specific to the offshore students? Could cross cultural cooperation help?
2   Establish whether two or more teachers with similar vision exist in the school with expertise in the same subject area.
3   Determine if effective communication is possible between the teachers (do they speak enough of a common language?).

4   Determine if personalities are suited for cooperation.
    Personality traits that CCTT members should possess include:
    •   flexibility
    •   confidence (especially for the teacher 'on show')
    •   open-mindedness
    •   cooperativeness.
5   Review the issues related to CCTTs and weigh the pros and cons of the proposed situation.
6   Request permission from administration (both Chinese and Canadian) for CCTT.
    •   Consider requesting support time to be built in to teachers' schedules for CCTT development.
7   Periodically reflect upon the progress of the CCTT and revise the model (if necessary).

My dissertation had far-reaching effects. In my school the model for Cross Cultural Teaching Teams was presented to the school staff, and I have been asked by a Canadian professor to publish the results further. I have gained both from the knowledge I explored, but also an increase in my professional confidence.

On a personal level the process of undertaking the dissertation had some unexpected outcomes for me. Contrary to my undergraduate experience, my MA in Geography Education excited me about learning. One of the most enjoyable aspects of the MA, and the dissertation in particular, was the treasure hunt of undertaking the literature review. Subsequently I found that engaging with research at this level was a challenge but a thoroughly enjoyable one. The support of my tutor was vital in helping me to overcome obstacles and challenging me to reflect critically on the work I was doing. Ultimately I felt a huge sense of achievement in completing the dissertation and a level of academic confidence I previously didn't have. From a professional perspective I found that undertaking specialist work in one area gave me sufficient background information that I felt more like an expert in my chosen field. This expertise may open doors to future opportunities. In fact, additional administrative responsibilities at work were offered to me within months of completing the dissertation.

What is a dissertation?

Bright and Leat (2000) note that many teachers have a tendency to disregard educational research due to perceived difficulties in applying the theoretical to classroom realities. Indeed, there is a tension in educational research between practical research and its theoretical value (see Williams 1998 for a discussion of practical versus theoretical research in geography education). Undertaking a dissertation is an important part of a Masters degree because it demonstrates independent work undertaken at a higher-degree level. Successful completion recognises an ability to conduct research to a post-graduate standard. Therefore completing a dissertation is more than just writing a long essay. It is an opportunity to undertake independent high-quality research into a field of your choice. This book provides dissertation summaries that give a flavour of what colleagues have chosen as suitable dissertation topics and how they have undertaken their research. Although each has adapted a structure that suits their own purpose, it is recognised that most dissertations include the following.

1   **Several pages that precede the introduction:** title page, abstract, acknowledgements, table of contents, list of figures and tables, and an explanation of abbreviations that may not be familiar to all readers.
2   **An introduction that sets the context for the research.** It also defines the scope and limits of the research. Who and what is it for? The introduction answers these questions.
3   **A literature review that both surveys and critically examines the existing literature** on your field of study. The literature review is like a frame in which your research sits. Put another way, it is a discussion of what we already know, what we think about what we 'know', and it serves as a launch pad for your research, which will venture beyond what we know or perhaps revisit what we think about what we 'know'.
4   **A chapter on research methods and methodology** that provides an overview of methods and methodologies in geography education research, discusses key considerations, and situates the dissertation within specific methodologies, strategies and research paradigms.
5   **A discussion, and justification, of the methods/design of your research.** Essentially this means describing what you did and explaining why you did it. Your design will have to stand up to scrutiny by the academics who will evaluate it.
6   **The findings of your research.** This chapter presents your data and a critical analysis it.
7   **A conclusion.** What does it all mean? What are the implications and limitations of your findings? What questions are left unanswered for future research?

There are many specialist texts on undertaking a research project and writing a dissertation, but it is even more useful to read a number of previous dissertations by students in your field, available from your institution's library and digital archives.

Practical advice

There are useful texts that offer practical support in how to structure and undertake your dissertation. The following were particularly useful to me:

*   Bolker's (1998) *Writing Your Dissertation in Fifteen Minutes a Day*.
*   Glatthorn and Joyner's (2005) *Writing the Winning Thesis or Dissertation*.

Managing your time

Effective time-management is imperative when undertaking a dissertation. Bolker's (1998) encouraging book title deliberately misleads the reader. Nevertheless, the message of the book title is clear; breaking down your dissertation into frequent but small chunks makes it an easily manageable task. Astute dissertation planners will create a schedule, or 'to-do' list with relatively firm deadlines. Inevitably, I missed many of the deadlines I set for myself; therefore building in weeks or even months of extra time is wise. Consider when you have holidays or extended slow periods at work or school and plan to be productive in these periods.

Balancing personal, family and work responsibilities may be the most difficult obstacle for people embarking on a Master's degree. It is imperative that you consider when you are able to complete the necessary work. A logical solution is establishing a schedule or routine, and to factor in time with family and friends. For me, early-morning work on weekends provided two distinct benefits. First, I got a sense of accomplishment so I could enjoy the rest of the weekend without guilt. Second, it was easier than working after a full day teaching. Consider also that dissertation work involves various tasks, some of which (like researching on the Internet) require less mental focus than others (for example, writing). Therefore, it is sensible to plan to write when you are well rested, whereas researching and formatting could be done while tired. Bear in mind that you are not a solitary individual. Without the support of your family, completing a dissertation is considerably more difficult so balancing everyone's needs is essential. You also need to consider your own health needs. Do not allow your dissertation to defer your exercise or sport regimen.

Researching

How do you gather and analyse data once your schedule is made? A decade ago, research was done primarily in your institution's library. Today the Internet has expanded research opportunity and flexibility. Google Scholar (www.scholar.google.com) proved invaluable as an Internet search engine that limits search results to academic journals and an Athens login access (provided with your university library card and account) gives access to many of the journals you will find online. However, your institution may not have complete subscriptions to some journals. Finding an article that looks especially good and relevant but that requires you to purchase a copy creates a frustrating dilemma: to spend money or go without needed literature? By and large, Internet research provides sufficient relevant literature that is both free and accessible from virtually anywhere in the world.

Once your research design is set and you have gathered data, analysing it creates another challenge. Quantitative data analysis was unfamiliar territory for me; I knew that numbers could be turned into graphs of various forms to illustrate meaning, but I relied on the help of several friends and colleagues from my math and science departments who guided me through using a spreadsheet and offered formulas and strategies. It is advisable to familiarise yourself with essential software prior to starting your dissertation if you expect to collect quantitative data.

The mountains of interview or observation data you may end up with also require analysis, which begins with coding,

> a simple process that everyone already knows how to do. For example, when you read a book, underline or highlight passages, and make margin notes you are 'coding' that book. Coding in [qualitative data analysis] is essentially the same thing.
>
> (Seidel 1998)

Software designed specifically to aid in analysing qualitative data is available. I settled on intuitive freeware called Weft QDA (available at www.pressure.to/qda/). Again, you are well-advised to plan ahead and experiment before starting the dissertation.

Writing up the dissertation

Initially, the length of the dissertation was the most daunting aspect of the whole thing. Ironically, the real problem became not how to write so much but how to cut down what I had written to meet the word-limit requirement. Strategies like deleting adjectives helped me to cut words and to make my writing sound more academic.

Writing each chapter may best be viewed as writing an essay (although you need not write chapters one to six consecutively – I wrote the sections that seemed easiest first). Hence, each chapter starts with an introduction and a thesis statement and finishes with a conclusion. It is very important to make clear to the reader where you are going and why. This 'sign posting' is especially important in a dissertation because of the long length. Even as the author I got lost in my manuscript, so it is not hard to imagine how difficult it can be for a reader of a dissertation.

Formatting the dissertation is a further challenge. What should a dissertation look like? Although dissertations differ, perusing a number of them will offer suggestions. Using a dissertation template (an Internet search should provide one for your preferred word processor) that clearly explained how to format a dissertation saves time and frustration from creating a consistently formatted document. The dissertation's list of references, which could easily contain upwards of 100 entries, further challenges the new researcher. Programs such as Endnote are designed to help and may also save time (available to download at www.endnote.com). Finding the right style sheet, the document that describes the specific conventions (font, size, spellings, etc.) required for publication at your institution, is equally important.

Seeking support

While you can be sure to receive invaluable feedback from your tutor, it is important that you are able to work independently. It may be that you cannot reach your tutor immediately due to holidays or other commitments. The dissertation requires considerable thought; therefore, it is imperative that you have someone or preferably several people to bounce ideas off and also for editing your writing. A word of caution is necessary here; do not assume that just because you have good friends or colleagues that they will spend the time to actually read and edit your writing. You are well advised to seek out supportive family, friends and colleagues before embarking on your dissertation.

Likewise, you require support from your school's administration if you are doing your dissertation and/or other Master's coursework while teaching. Support from administrators may vary from cool acceptance of your research to ecstatic enthusiasm. Regardless, it is essential that you seek permission and be upfront and open about your research and data collection from the beginning with administration, colleagues and students (see Cohen and Manion 2007 for a discussion of ethics in education research).

Once the dissertation is written up, one is still left with the very difficult challenge of judging the quality of what has been written. McElroy's (1993) paper, 'How can we be sure? Ground rules for judging research quality', serves as a checklist for the researcher/writer and makes clear the extent that ethics in research needs to be considered (also see the discussion of Frankfort–Nachmias and Nachmias' cost–benefit ratio in Cohen and Manion 2007) and how it is necessary to justify one's research approach (again, see Cohen and Manion 2007). Other key documents that provide support are found in the annotated reference list at the end of this chapter.

Undertaking research as part of professional practice

Alison Leonard

David Mitchell (2005) 'Curriculum Innovation Through Continuing Professional Development: the Local Solutions Approach'

Research in education is not just limited to the work undertaken for dissertations. Local Solutions, a Geographical Association (GA) curriculum development project, was researched and reported as part of David Mitchell's MA dissertation. The project sought to involve teachers in local groups to engage with curriculum-making activities. Mitchell's dissertation has been chosen as it demonstrates many of the benefits gained from engagement in the research process. The research was also reported in a *Geography* article (Mitchell 2006) which explains: 'Local Solutions is an approach to curriculum development developed by the GA to support creative teachers at a time when school geography in the UK is under pressure.' 'Local Solutions' (LS) is a distinctive approach to curriculum innovation through the continuing professional development (CPD) of geography teachers. Mitchell's work focuses on one LS project: 'Making the most of a department intranet.'

In the introduction, which includes his literature review, Mitchell identifies obstacles facing teachers who seek to innovate and take risks in the classroom, and warns of the difficulties in communicating and diffusing curriculum developments to a wider audience. However, quoting extensively throughout his dissertation from Sachs (2003) he also acknowledges a range of benefits when such 'transformational professionalism' occurs, including substantial improvements in teaching and learning. He notes how the process of engaging in collaborative research can have real benefits, like seeking to create an engaging, relevant, innovative geography curriculum in departments that currently appear resistant to such change, where innovation is viewed as a threat. In this section, he also reflects on the importance of the role of the Subject Association, the GA, in the process of curriculum development.

For his action-research methodology, Mitchell ensured that the three factors McElroy (1980) had identified as determining successful outcomes from CPD were built into his research: sensitivity by the trainer, a lengthy or prolonged period of engagement and, ideally, a minimum of two participants from each of the seven participating schools.

Using a case study strategy, seeking an exploratory, interpretative approach and 'thick description' of this LS project, Mitchell used a 'hybrid approach' (2005: 38) to his methodology. Since Mitchell was the project leader for this GA LS project, he was able to carry out his research with a 'built-in evaluation mechanism'. Only one of his data sources, research diaries written by participating teachers, were external to the GA project and required for research purposes only. Mitchell obviates some limitations of his methodology, such as his position as researcher and project leader, by using triangulation. However, he notes that the limited duration of the two school-based action-research elements of his study did not adequately allow for its 'impacts on learning' to be measured.

In analysing the results Mitchell sought to review two sets of outcomes: curriculum developments and CPD for participating geography teachers. He presents these in tabular form, identifying six for the former, primarily student-oriented and ten for the latter, three relating to participants' ICT skills, four to networking opportunities. Additionally he provides a summary of why the seven participating schools took part at the outset of the project in 2004, demonstrating that research participants can have a diversity of intended curriculum-development outcomes. Mitchell also draws on the project's external evaluator's report.

In his conclusion, Mitchell offers insights into the importance of the role of senior managers, emphasising that this could have a significant effect for individuals working on the project. He warns that the relative fragility of the LS process is a weakness, but for those 'activist professionals' whom he suggests should be working in similar LS projects, the process can succeed. Those geography teachers working in contexts that allow them to make innovative changes should take heart from his findings, while those managing such individuals can facilitate or frustrate this 'transformative professionalism'.

Much emphasis is placed on the role of e-learning and integrating ICT in the curriculum; Mitchell's dissertation is important because it demonstrates that websites can enable pupils' learning, teachers can benefit by collaboration and outcomes can be affected by colleagues' support. While 'resistors to change' can frustrate, positive innovations and a wealth of pioneering changes can accrue from creative, innovative teachers. Mitchell's work highlights the importance of 'activist professionals' and the value of working collaboratively within school departments, which can support those seeking to innovate and strengthen the place of geography in the curriculum.

The research identifies the importance of this process of curriculum development: one that is locally situated and responsive to local contexts. However, the outcomes of the research are also valuable for others. Dissemination was a key part of the Local Solutions projects and Mitchell notes:

> The dissemination process was at an early stage, with the publications and face to face dissemination still to take place. However, there was evidence that the web materials were of significant interest to Geography teachers. In the first three weeks of their being posted on the GA website, the 'Intranets' project site, under the title 'A department website' was viewed 385 times, making it the second most popular project on the site during that time.
>
> (Mitchell 2005: 87)

Additionally as a result of taking part in the LS project in one of the participating schools, teachers developed an independent relationship with OUP publishers, 'piloting new OUP learning support materials accessed through a safe portal so that pupils could access materials from home' (Mitchell 2005).

Again Mitchell's MA dissertation exemplifies other benefits for pupils when their teachers engage in the research process specifically related to e-learning. He found that pupils were more motivated and produced more effective coursework in the majority of schools taking part, while other reported benefits included more independent learning. The project's external evaluator also supported these observations.

By engagement in the research process, teachers can gain in a variety of ways. The most commonly reported CPD outcomes from this project were higher motivation amongst staff, a closer working relationship with the Subject Association and a more critical approach to applying ICT. Involvement in the project also meant that schools started sharing resources and reported an ethos shift in the geography department. Mitchell claimed that the latter two outcomes are 'indicative of sustained CPD', and concluded that there is evidence of CPD beyond those directly involved, which Mitchell referred to as 'informal or "organic" dissemination'.

Finally, Mitchell's work was written up as a Masters dissertation, the research included other participants who contributed to the project. His conclusions show that the effects of the research have had a positive impact on the participants' professional development.

Further reading

1 Bolker, J. (1998) *Writing Your Dissertation in Fifteen Minutes a Day: a Guide to Starting, Revising, and Finishing Your Doctoral Thesis.* Henry Holt and Company, New York. This book is a valuable resource for those dissertation writers who are struggling with the writing aspect.
2 Cohen, L. and Manion, L. (2007) *Research Methods in Education.* Routledge, London. This is essential reading for a Masters level student and should be reviewed when planning for a dissertation.
3 Glatthorn, A. and Joyner, R. (2005) *Writing the Winning Thesis or Dissertation: a Step-by-Step Guide.* Corwin Press, Thousand Oaks. This book provides practical advice for all stages of the dissertation.
4 McElroy, B. (1993) 'How can we be sure? Ground rules for judging research quality', *International Research in Geographical and Environmental Education* 2, 1, pp. 66–69. This article provides an essential checklist for the dissertation writer to judge their own work.

References

Bassey, M. (1999) *Case Study Research in Educational Settings.* Open University Press, Buckingham.

Bolker, J. (1998) *Writing Your Dissertation in Fifteen Minutes a Day: a Guide to Starting, Revising, and Finishing Your Doctoral Thesis.* Henry Holt and Company, New York.

Bright, N. and Leat, D. (2000) 'Towards a new professionalism', in W.A. Kent (ed.), *Reflective Practice in Geography Teaching.* Paul Chapman Publishing, London.

Cohen, L. and Manion, L. (2007) *Research Methods in Education.* Routledge, London.

Gerber, R. and Williams, M. (2000) 'Overview and international perspectives', in W.A. Kent (ed.) *Reflective Practice in Geography Teaching.* Paul Chapman Publishing, London.

Glatthorn, A. and Joyner, R. (2005) *Writing the Winning Thesis or Dissertation: a Step-by-Step Guide.* Corwin Press, Thousand Oaks.

Kent, A. (1996) 'Facilitating research in geographical and environmental education', in Williams, M. (ed.) *Understanding Geographical and Environmental Education.* Cassell, London.

McElroy, B. (1980) 'School based curriculum development: an investigation into teachers' perceptions of their role', unpublished dissertation for MA Geography in Education, Institute of Education, University of London.

McElroy, B. (1993) 'How can we be sure? Ground rules for judging research quality', *International Research in Geographical and Environmental Education*, 2, 1, pp. 66–69.

Mitchell, D. (2006) 'Local Solutions': an approach to curriculum development in geography', *Geography*, 91, 2, pp. 150–158.

Roberts, M. (2000) 'The role of research in supporting teaching and learning', in W.A. Kent (ed.) *Reflective Practice in Geography Teaching.* Paul Chapman Publishing, London.

Sachs, J. (2003) *The Activist Teaching Profession.* Open University Press, Maidenhead.

Seidel, J. (1998) 'Qualitative data analysis'. Online, available at: www.qualisresearch.com/qda_paper.htm.

Training and Development Agency for Schools (n.d.) *Masters in Teaching and Learning*. Online, available at: www.tda.gov.uk/leaders/teachers/mtl.aspx.

Williams, M. (1998) 'Review of research in geographical education', in W.A. Kent (ed.) *Research Forum 1: Textbooks*. Institute of Education, London: University of London.

13 Writing at Masters level

Clare Brooks

For many teachers, undertaking Masters level work in the field of education will require a new type of writing. Even if you have been successful at under-graduate or post-graduate level, you may find that assignments required for Masters level courses in education are different. This chapter will help you to consider what the issues are for writing at this level and how you can address them.

The aims of this chapter are:

- to explore what writing at Masters level requires.
- to examine different types of writing and how they can help professional practice.
- to share some strategies for improving writing at Masters level.

What is different about writing at this level?

Whatever the focus of your assignments, or the guidance that you have been given by your university, the standard of what counts as Masters level work has been pre-determined by the Quality Assurance Agency for Higher Education (or QAA) (2008). It is the role of the QAA to ensure that standards across higher-education levels are consistent. Their guidelines for Masters level are laid out in Box 13.1.

Box 13.1 Descriptor for a higher education qualification at level 7: Masters degree

Masters degrees are awarded to students who have demonstrated:

- a systematic understanding of knowledge, and a critical awareness of current problems and/or new insights, much of which is at, or informed by, the forefront of their academic discipline, field of study or area of professional practice
- a comprehensive understanding of techniques applicable to their own research or advanced scholarship

---

- originality in the application of knowledge, together with a practical understanding of how established techniques of research and enquiry are used to create and interpret knowledge in the discipline
- conceptual understanding that enables the student:
  - to evaluate critically current research and advanced scholarship in the discipline
  - to evaluate methodologies and develop critiques of them and, where appropriate, to propose new hypotheses.

Typically, holders of the qualification will be able to:

- deal with complex issues both systematically and creatively, make sound judgements in the absence of complete data, and communicate their conclusions clearly to specialist and non-specialist audiences
- demonstrate self-direction and originality in tackling and solving problems, and act autonomously in planning and implementing tasks at a professional or equivalent level
- continue to advance their knowledge and understanding, and to develop new skills to a high level.

And holders will have:

- the qualities and transferable skills necessary for employment requiring:
  - the exercise of initiative and personal responsibility
  - decision-making in complex and unpredictable situations
  - the independent learning ability required for continuing professional development.

(Taken from QAA 2008)

This benchmark applies to all courses assessed at this level, and your course will have undertaken a strict validation procedure in order to ensure that it meets these criteria. In addition, each Higher Education Institution will have interpreted the QAA benchmarks and produced their own criteria for what constitutes Masters level work. These should be made available to all students.

In some universities, Masters level criteria, or how your work is assessed, may have been reworked to reflect the unique nature of the PGCE, incorporating both professional and academic criteria. PGCE courses are different to other Masters-accredited courses as they are also professional qualifications. Therefore part of the assessment of a PGCE relates to professional practice, for example the Standards for Qualified Teacher Status (QTS). But the Standards for QTS are different to the focus of Masters level criteria. A PGCE course will have designed assignments to either provide evidence that you have met the Standards for QTS, or as evidence that you have met Masters level criteria, or indeed both. It is important to know by which criteria an assignment is being judged.

What, then, makes Masters level work different?

To understand the significance of Masters level study, it is useful to remember the roots of Masters qualification in British universities. The three traditional levels of qualifications were: Bachelor degrees, Master degrees and Doctoral degrees. Bachelors degrees were considered to indicate a good general education. Masters degrees were a licence to practise. Similar to the craftsmen's guilds, obtaining a Masters degree was viewed as a rite of passage to becoming a better-informed, more authoritative figure in the field. To reach the next level of PhD or Doctorate required the demonstration of new knowledge in the field (Phillips and Pugh 1994). In this way, rather than becoming a reporter of other people's research, the 'Doctors' were also able to contribute to the development of the field. Each level was assessed by colleagues, and candidates had to demonstrate that they met the required level for the degree to be awarded.

As the 2008 QAA framework for Masters level work indicates, qualification at this level requires:

- being able to draw upon the literature in the field;
- being able to reflect on this literature and how it may affect practice;
- being able to synthesise the theory and the practice and in doing so to be able to show originality of thought and argument.

At undergraduate level, much work is a synthesis of what has gone on before. Students are required to read widely, to be able to synthesise the literature and to be able to use it in response to an essay or coursework question. In geography, either as social or physical science, undergraduates are also required to conduct research of their own and to present this either as part of an essay or in a report. For most undergraduates this will have been the main focus of their dissertation.

Working at Masters level on a PGCE requires a detailed understanding of the field of education in a similar way to undergraduate work, but with some differences. Candidates are expected to have a more authoritative understanding of the field, and to be able to situate themselves within it and to understand how it applies to professional practice. This means demonstrating knowledge of the field interwoven with 'evidence' from practice. In the best cases, literature and practice come together and can throw up new insights for both. The writer and reader will feel that they have a deeper and more informed understanding of both the literature and the practice as a result of having engaged with the work. If that feels like a tall order, then that will be because it is! A Masters degree is not easy, but is well worth striving for.

It is common for teachers to feel a degree of discomfort in using their professional practice and experience in this way. Some teachers feel that their observations are inadequate, particularly when used to critique literature on established theories. They may also feel that they are only a novice in the field and not 'qualified' to criticise others. At university, students are generally encouraged to be as 'objective' as possible, and to write assignments as though they are impartial observations. Writing in the first person can feel uncomfortable, as can describing a classroom-based incident as evidence to support your argument. This can be because, as geography graduates, PGCE students have been schooled in a particular type of academic discourse. Writing on the PGCE requires a different approach, one which the rest of this chapter will explore.

Writing as a thinking tool

Before moving onto specific issues of writing at Masters level, the follow section explores writing as a thinking tool. Research into the work of academics demonstrates that successful academics don't just write for publication but view writing as an important part of the thinking and creative process.

In Chapter 3, Sheila King describes how diaries and journals can help to develop reflective practice. The emphasis is not just on recording and describing incidences, but in thinking and responding to critical questions. This is similar to an approach promoted by Julia Cameron (2000) to promote creativity. By allowing writers to explore their thoughts on paper, new connections and new ideas can come to the fore. Murray (2005) describes this in an academic context as 'free-writing'. Murray suggests that the process of free-writing, without focusing on writing conventions, can help writers to overcome barriers and to unleash their creativity. She argues that professional knowledge constitutes knowledge, experiences, thoughts, conversations and feelings. Free-writing can help to illuminate fruitful connections between them.

Murray's approach is to write continuously, for at least five minutes, without pausing for corrections, reviewing or even inserting punctuation, and without worrying about how it reads. Murray describes this as intellectual development, and recommends it as a useful way of overcoming writer's block or to start a writing task. Free-writing can help to identify an angle or an argument for an assignment.

Recording experience as evidence

When preparing academic assignments, students are often required to use evidence to support their assertions. However, it is not always clear what is meant by and what counts as evidence in education research. Richard Andrews explores this very issue in his short paper, 'What counts as evidence in education research?' (2007). In this paper he notes that evidence and data are not the same thing. There is already a huge body of existing evidence available through research literature already published. Andrews argues that work in education should always begin by doing a thorough review of what has already been published in the field. Beyond that, Andrews argues for a liberal definition of evidence, one that embraces personal transformation, and that can draw up a variety of methods and data, including observations. Ultimately, he argues that what you choose to use for evidence will be determined by what question you are asking and answering.

This presents a powerful case as to why what teachers experience, through practice, can be used as valuable evidence in assignments. It is important, however, to also appreciate the scope of this evidence. Just because something happened once, in one lesson, does not mean it is a generalisable truth for all scenarios. However, if the appropriate analysis is applied, classroom episodes and experiences can be valuable evidence to support a point.

Writing issues

Once you have decided what it is that you wish to write, the next challenge is to adopt the appropriate academic tone. Giltrow (2002) recommends that the best way to achieve this is to become acquainted with the appropriate academic discourse in your field. In practice, this means reading examples of other assignments, and the assignment guidelines generated by your institution. Giltrow (2002) recommends different levels of reading here. The initial reading may be for content. On a second reading, focus specifically on stylistic features, such as the use of citation, inclusion of evidence, the voice of the author and how the argument develops. A third reading can go even further, looking at paragraph structure, word use and signposts through the essay. This is not about plagiarism but acquainting yourself with the accepted academic practice in your field.

Academic tone

Here is an example of a piece of writing, taken from the introduction of an assignment on sustainability, which just hasn't quite got the academic tone right:

> In an epoch of existential knowledge, where shift happens and acceptance of universal altruism is a millennium goal given, we have moved on from isolated geographical antecedents of environmental science and social justice to find a modern day synergetic geography defended by global citizens in the arena of sustainability.

First, you might notice that the whole paragraph is just one sentence. There are too many clauses and it is easy for the reader to get lost in what the author is trying to say. The language is also complicated, which obfuscates the meaning. The reader is left with a general idea of what the author means, but still a little confused about certain points. For instance, what does the author mean by 'acceptance of universal altruism is a millennium goal given'? It feels as though the author has deliberately used big words to 'sound clever'! More simple expression would actually get the point across in a stronger way.

Compare the above extract to the following, also from a PGCE assignment, which has got the tone right:

> A nuanced approach to a place-specific unit is also recommended by writers such as Massey (2006), especially in order to expose the 'multiple geographies' which can be found within countries. She argues that 'places are meeting places of different people, different groups, different ethnicities' (ibid.: 50). Both Massey (2006) and Brooks & Morgan (2006) argue that when examining the development levels of a country it is easy to fall into the trap of simplification. Regional differences can cloud the picture. Simple labels such as 'Less Economically Developed' or 'More Economically Developed' mask the inherent contradictions within a country.

In this extract, the sentences are shorter, and more simply constructed. The author has used evidence (from other sources) to substantiate his point. The message is powerfully portrayed and easily understood. The reader is left clear as to what the author wants to say.

An important dimension of academic tone is the words that you use. The next paragraph is extracted from a student's assignment followed by my rewritten version that trims the paragraph of unnecessary words but without destroying the meaning:

> There was clear progression in learning in the sequence of lessons. In each lesson the pupils built on what they had learnt in the previous lessons. For example, in lesson 2, pupils learnt about the different types of development indicators and they were introduced to new geographical terms (e.g. GDP, life expectancy and infant mortality) that they would need to understand for their assessment (lesson 5) and later on in the unit to understand more complex concepts. Figure 2 below is an example of a pupils work from lesson 2. As pupils had to determine whether an indicator would be higher in an MEDC or LEDC and explain two of their answers this shows understanding of the indicators.
>
> (118 words)

> In the sequence, progression was build into the planning between lessons and also within each lesson. For example, the geographical terminology and development indicators taught in Lesson two were developed into more complex concepts later in the unit, and assessed in lesson 5. As Figure 2 shows this student was able to use the terminology correctly and understand its meaning.
>
> (60 words)

Students often use the unnecessary terminology to try to make their work sound academic. Ross-Larson (1996) calls this 'fat' and suggests, for clear writing, these should be removed (see Table 13.1):

Table 13.1 Examples of 'fat'

'Fat'	Replace with
in the field of physical geography	physical geography
the process of teaching	teaching
the amount of work	the work
the case of one student	one student
the concept of sustainability	sustainability

Source: Ross-Larson (1996).

Ross-Larsen (1996) also suggests cutting out weak modifiers from your writing such as:

- actually
- carefully
- very
- in fact
- definitely
- particularly
- relatively (see Ross-Larsen 1996 for a full list).

A common mistake that students make in their writing is to include big words or redundant phrases to try to make their work sound more 'academic'. There are also some stock phrases that students often use which can give the reader the wrong impression! For instance, Table 13.2, taken from Rugg and Petre (2004), illustrates a list of commonly used phrases and what the reader thinks they really mean.

First person versus third person

In most undergraduate courses, students are encouraged to write in the third person. This effectively removes the writer's 'voice' from the piece and makes it sound more authoritative and objective. There are academic genres that prefer the third person for professional and academic work. There are others who suggest that one can never claim to be truly objective, and so, particularly when writing about personal experience, it is important to allow the author's voice to be present. It is useful to look through old assignments to get a flavour of which approach is preferred by your institution. I would suggest that when writing about personal experience the first person always sounds more powerful.

Tenses

Many novice and experienced writers can get caught up with changing in tenses in the middle of their writing. The dilemma comes in the difference

Table 13.2 Reading between the lines: some classic examples

You say ...	Others read this as meaning ...
Smith says...	I haven't read many journal articles
... explains Dr Smith ...	I've read too many magazines
... enthuses Dr Smith ...	I've read too much Barbara Cartland
There is some general consensus that (a) ...	... there is some agreement that ...
There is some general consensus that (b) ...	I don't have any specific references but this sounds like a plausible claim.
It is clear that ...	I think ...
It is arguable that ...	I hope ...
A larger sample might prove ...	I don't understand anything about inferential statistics or survey methods.
A recent study found that ...	I don't have a reference for this, but I'm fairly sure it's true.
There is some anecdotal evidence that ...	Some people in a bar told me that ...

Source: Extract from *Reading between the lines: some classic examples*, Rugg, G. and Petre, M. (2004) *The Unwritten Rules of PhD Research* Open University Press 2004, Table 3, p. 123.

between 'doing' your work, and 'writing' your work. For instance, whilst you may have taught the lesson some weeks ago, you may choose to write about it in the present tense in your assignment. You may also wish to refer to published work in the present tense, but your experience in the past. Giltrow (2002) notes that academic authors often only use the past tense to reflect an out-dated argument that has been superseded. Most prefer to use the present tense throughout. The golden rule is to decide on which tense you wish to use and to stick to it throughout your work.

Paragraphs

In my experience, when teachers start to write assignments, they can get carried away with the flow of what they are writing and forget to pay attention to its structure. If you are finding it difficult to get across what it is you want to say then I would recommend paying close attention to each paragraph. What follows below may seem formulaic and mechanical, but it is worth checking your writing to ensure that it follows certain conventions of paragraph structure.

• Decide on what you want each paragraph to say – there should be one main idea in each paragraph.

- Summarise the message of your paragraph into a topic sentence – this can become the first sentence of your paragraph.
- The following sentences in your paragraph need to support that topic sentence – you may include here a reference from the literature, or a reflection from your own practice or one from each. These sentences explain your topic sentence.
- The last sentence in the paragraph explains the significance of your topic sentence and prepares the link to the next paragraph.

You should find that once each paragraph has a clear structure and meaning, it is fairly straightforward to link them together to ensure that the argument in your assignment flows. A key strategy to use here is to read your work aloud. If you stumble across sentences or phrases, then they probably need to be rewritten.

Using citations

Universities have specific guidelines about citations and may offer advice on how to use them correctly. I would strongly recommend that you pay detailed attention to these. Many universities prefer the Harvard system. In this system work is cited in the text, and included in a reference list at the end of the essay, as has been done throughout this book. Again, it is important to check your institution's guidelines on how they wish citations to be used.

Some key questions are when to use a citation or not. This has to be considered extremely carefully, as incorrect citations can lead to your work being considered as plagiarised, which can carry strict penalties. The yardstick about citations is quite easy, however; if you are using someone else's work then it is important to cite where it has come from and to clearly direct the reader to where they can find the original. It is useful to see citations as a kind of shorthand to help the reader to follow-up on where your evidence has come from. Citations are not, however, a substitute for fully explaining your point or letting the reader in on what you are thinking. You still need to explain what you are citing whilst ensuring that the reader is clear whose original work it was.

Citation is extremely important to ensure that your work is not suspected of plagiarism. Plagiarism is taken extremely seriously by universities. It is generally understood as taking and using other people's work, either intentionally or unintentionally. It is the students' responsibility to ensure that their work is properly cited throughout so that the reader (or examiner) is clear that all references to others' work are correctly cited. Even if you paraphrase work from another author, it is important to acknowledge where the idea came from, so that your work is not accused of plagiarism. It is also worth checking out your institution's policies and guidelines.

Using citations correctly is also very important for instilling confidence in the reader and, when used well, will directly show the reader the originality in your own work.

And finally ...

Writing at Masters level is both extremely challenging and extremely reward-ing. Feedback from my students indicates that, whilst many find it to be hard work, the benefits are unexpected. The process of writing about teaching, and particularly classroom experiences, means putting into words some things that teachers can take for granted. It can illuminate assumptions or generalisa-tions that you hadn't anticipated. It can raise questions, and by exploring the literature and reflecting on practice, it can help you to answer those ques-tions. That is why writing at Masters level will do more than help you to get Masters level qualifications, but should also help you to become a better geo-graphy teacher.

For discussion

- Review your own writing. What are the common problems that you encounter? What feedback have you had about your writing? Use this as a way of alerting yourself to areas where you need to get help (see Further reading).
- Read a selection of successful assignments alongside the grade criteria. Can you see how the criteria has been used? Now compare your own draft to the criteria – what do you need to do to improve your work?
- Give your work to a colleague to read, or read it out loud. A general rule of thumb is that if a sentence makes your/your colleague stumble, it needs to be re-written!

Further reading

Your first port-of-call should be to check out the guidelines and support available at your institution. Be clear on any writing advice and recommendations given, which criteria are being used for your assignment, and read as many examples of successful pieces that you can.

For good general advice on writing and editing, and developing academic literacy:

1 Billingham, J. (2002) *Editing and Revising Text*. Oxford: Oxford University Press.
2 Craswell, G. (2005) *Writing for Academic Success: a Postgraduate Guide*. London: Sage.
3 Giltrow, J. (2002) *Academic Writing: Writing and Reading in the Disciplines*, 3rd edn. Toronto: Broadview Press.
4 Peck, J. and Coyle, M. (2005) *The Student's Guide to Writing: Grammar, Punctuation and Spelling*, 2nd edn. Basingstoke: Palgrave.
5 Ross-Larsen, B. (1996) *Edit Yourself*. New York: W.W. Norton & Company.
6 Zinsser, W. (2006) *On Writing Well*. New York: Collins (but only the earlier chapters).

References

Andrews, R. (2007) 'What counts as evidence in Education?' TTRB. Online, avail-able at: www.ttrb.ac.uk/attachments/38ba1867-f5d9–4c5f-943c-3218a7399724.pdf.

Bell, J. (1993) *Doing Your Research Project*. Buckingham: Open University Press.

Cameron, J. (2000) *The Right to Write*. London: Putnam Publishing Group

Giltrow, J. (2002) *Academic Writing: Writing and Reading in the Disciplines*. Ormskirk: Broadview.

Murray, R. (2005) *Writing for Academic Journals*. Maidenhead: Open University Press.

Phillips, E.M. and Pugh, D.S. (1994) *How to Get a PhD: a Handbook for Students and their Supervisors*. Buckingham: Open University Press.

QAA (2008) *The Framework for Higher Education Qualifications in England, Wales and Northern Ireland*. QAA 264 08/08.

Ross-Larsen, B. (1996) *Edit Yourself*. New York: W.W. Norton & Company.

Rugg, G. and Petre, M. (2004) *The Unwritten Rules of PhD Research*. Maidenhead: Open University Press.

Zinsser, W. (2006) *On Writing Well*. New York: Collins.

Index